STRATEGIC PLANNING

MANAGEMENT WITHIN
THE LOCAL CHURCH

J. HILARY GBOTOE, JR.

Copyright © 2024 J. Hilary Gbotoe, Jr.

All rights reserved. No part of this book may be reproduced, stored, or transmitted by any means—whether auditory, graphic, mechanical, or electronic—without written permission of both publisher and author, except in the case of brief excerpts used in critical articles and reviews. Unauthorized reproduction of any part of this work is illegal and is punishable by law.

ISBN: 979-8-89419-212-3 (sc)
ISBN: 979-8-89419-213-0 (hc)
ISBN: 979-8-89419-214-7 (e)

Because of the dynamic nature of the Internet, any web addresses or links contained in this book may have changed since publication and may no longer be valid. The views expressed in this work are solely those of the author and do not necessarily reflect the views of the publisher, and the publisher hereby disclaims any responsibility for them.

One Galleria Blvd., Suite 1900, Metairie, LA 70001
(504) 702-6708

CONTENTS

Dedication vii

Acknowledgements ix

Preface xi

Introduction xv

Chapter 1 Strategic Management: A Need
           in the Local Church 1
           Denominationalism and Strategic
                Leadership in the Local Church 6
           What Does It Mean to Create Meaning? 9

Chapter 2 A Perspective on the Historical
           Development of Leadership Models 19
           A Historical Overview of the
                Leadership Models 19
           Preclassical Era Leadership Model 20
           Classical Era Leadership Model 21
           Modernism Leadership Model 23
           Postmodernism Leadership Model 24
           Philosophy and Organizational
                Development 25
           Traditional/Conventional Models
                Embodied in Philosophy 26
           Traditional/Conventional Theories
                Embodied in Philosophy 26
           Culture and Organizational Development 28

	Traditional/Conventional Models Embodied in Culture 29
	Reflection 29
	Lessons We Can Learn from the Historical Perspective on Leadership Models 30
	Definition of Deconstruction 33
	Deconstructing Leadership as Influence 33
	Deconstructing Leadership as Motivation 34
	Deconstructing Leadership as Partnership ... 34
	Conclusion 35

Chapter 3   Data Mining and Analysis: A Guide to Practical and Reasonable Strategic Plan 36

           Understanding Data Collection 38

           Methods of Data Collection 41

           Data Mining and Analysis 43

           Data Mining and Collaboration 43

           Data collection and Analysis 45

           Database 46

Chapter 4   The Impact of Strategic Planning on the Local Church 48

           The Role of Innovation in Strategic Management 48

           Leadership 49

           People 50

           Basic Values 52

           Innovation Values 54

           My Years as Senior Pastor of the Monrovia Open Bible Church in Liberia (1992–1999) 56

	Initial Phase of KHM (1999–2004) 58
	Benefits of Strategic Management within the Local Church 60
	Domestic and Global Outreaches 64
Chapter 5	Understanding Organizational Paradigms and Adapting to Maximize Relevancy in a Postmodern World 72
	An Overview of Current Organizational Paradigms 73
	The Rational System 73
	The Natural System 74
	The Open System 74
	Strategic Management and Organizational Paradigm 75
Chapter 6	Strategy Formulations and Implementations ... 83
	Environmental Analysis 85
	Long-Term Objectives 86
Chapter 7	Developing a Winning Strategic Plan 93
	The Influence of Organizational Culture on Developing a Strategic Plan .. 93
	The Role of the Senior Pastor in the Development of the Strategic Plan 94
	Challenges in Developing a Winning Strategic Plan 95
	Principles to Consider in Developing the Strategic Plan 96
	Understanding the Grand Strategy Clusters 101
	The Importance of Developing a Strategic Road Map 101

Developing Kingdom Harvest
 Ministries Inc. Liberia Strategic Plan....102
Adapting the Five Principles of
 Strategic Planning into KHM
 Strategic Plan..108
Interpreting the Matched Pair
 Analysis of KHM 114
The Grand Strategy Cluster Matrix 117
KHM's Strategic Road Map 121

Bibliography..127

DEDICATION

With humility and honor, I dedicate this book to all pastors and church leaders who are putting in their best efforts despite the many challenges.

I also dedicate this book, with gratitude and love, to my parents. Their steadfast faith in God coupled with their commitment to have their children (five boys, four girls) obtain quality education is amazing. Dad and Mom, you are the best. You gave beyond your means so we can become what we are today.

Lastly, but far from the least, I dedicate this book to all my children, family members, and friends who stood with me during trying times and encouraged me to continue to press on. I love you all. I owe a debt of gratitude to you all for believing in me, believing in the vision the Lord has given to me, and making yourselves available in whatever way you could to make the book a reality. Thanks and God bless.

ACKNOWLEDGEMENTS

I would like to acknowledge all those who in some ways contributed to the success of this book. Space will not allow me to name everyone, but your efforts and encouragements are noted. To Mandy Keef for the excellent work of editing the manuscript. I appreciate your thoughtfulness, thoroughness, critiques, and positive feedback. To my friends who read the manuscript and encouraged me to publish, thank you for believing in me. To my lovely, beautiful, and most compassionate wife, Euphemia Dennis Gbotoe, for putting up with me and pushing me to continue no matter the challenges. Thank you all for your patience and love.

PREFACE

This book is the product of critical analysis and investigations. About 250 churches were surveyed within a period of two years. The idea of the survey was initially based upon research needed to help empower struggling churches.

The 250 churches had membership ranging from fifty to four hundred people. The churches surveyed were from all denominations (Catholic and Protestants) and ethnicity. 10 percent of the churches surveyed were Catholics, 20 percent non-evangelical Protestants, and 70 percent evangelical Protestants. 35 percent of the churches surveyed were within rural communities, 40 percent within the suburb of urban communities, and 25 percent within urban communities. 55 percent of the churches surveyed considered themselves to be of mixed ethnicity, 15 percent was all white, while 20 percent were of African immigrant ethnicity, and 10 percent were Hispanic.

Of the 250 churches surveyed, about 12 percent had some form of written plan for church growth.

About 79 percent had never thought about a strategic plan or given the idea serious consideration. 12 churches claimed to have explored the idea but never formally drafted or finalized a written strategic plan. What was most shocking to me was that about 78 percent of the lead pastors of the churches surveyed had either a master's degree or higher. About 15 percent of the pastors had obtained a bachelor degree, and only 7 percent did not have a formal college degree.

From the statistics above, lack of formal education is not a challenge in the US-based churches as compared to churches in Africa and around the world. So why is the church in America not growing? Why is it that every research highlight local churches in America are closing their doors at an alarming rate? This book seeks to address a major (not the only) solution to this problem. There must be an *intentional* strategic plan developed and implemented by each local church that challenges common assumptions (not one handed down by a denominational hierarchy as discussed later).

Also, each local pastor must intentionally and honestly deconstruct his/her leadership style with the goal of becoming a leader that can proactively minister to the needs of each person within the community in which the church is located (more on deconstructing leadership style discussed further in the book).

It is time that church leaders become critical thinkers that do not just gather information but focus on information in a way that stimulates deep probing. In fact, critical thinking can be classified as the outcome of deep inquiries coupled with careful analysis and evaluation of facts (Ruggiero, 2004). Kirby and Goodpaster (2002), argued that what gives a critical thinker or writer "clarity, exactness, awareness, [and] richness" (p. 7) is his/ her ability to think creatively. Thus, my message to pastors and church leaders is that it is time to shift our leadership approach for better coordination and enhanced proficiency. We can do this by making full use of our God-given creativity and critical thinking skills.

Great thinkers often influence society to challenge common assumptions, thereby enhancing the manner of lifestyle and transforming the communities. In every age, from the preclassical to postmodern era, critical thinkers had spiked innovations by challenging traditional thought patterns. For example, it was critical thinking that gave birth to the Protestant Reformation. Critical thinking is most often the offspring of creative thinking. According to Kirby and Goodpaster (2002), creative thinking is the "ability to look at one thing and see another" (p. 113). Creativity is important to the critical thinker because by being creative, thinkers can properly organize their thoughts in a manner that is stimulating and insightful. Critical thoughts spring from creativity, logical reasoning, analysis, and investigations. In essence, critical thinking involves evaluating information in an analytical manner with the goal of making judgment and conclusions that can lead to innovation as well as challenge common assumptions. There is a need for great thinker in the body of Christ today.

INTRODUCTION

The world is experiencing many challenges today apparently more than any time in the history of mankind. Businesses are failing and going bankrupt. Politicians cannot agree upon what is best for their people and countries. Governments around the world are going bankrupt due to corrupt leadership and depleted natural resources. Financial institutions are failing miserably due to greed and unethical practices. Uncertainty is prevailing within every sector of society and industry. Unprecedented unemployment seems to be the norm around the world.

More disturbing than the challenges the world is encountering is the fact that the church is seemingly less attractive to the world. According to the American Religion Identification Survey (2008), professing Christians in the United States declined from 86 percent in 1990 to 77 percent in 2001. Olson (2008) in his groundbreaking research of over 200,000 churches declares that about 3,707 churches closed their doors each year between 2000 to 2005. According to the Keep God in America website (2010), 3,500 to 4,000 churches are closed each year in America with a sharp decline in Sunday attendance. To make matter worse, The church (Catholic and Protestant, evangelical and nonevangelical, Anglican and Orthodox) is hit on every side with scandals. To add to the shock, some pastors and bishops are declaring that they are gay and lesbian. Some denominations are split over the ordination of gay and lesbian bishops. The question then is, can the church be relevant in a world full of challenges and problems.

This book seeks to answer the question about the relevancy of the church in a troubling world. However, this book is not about the debate over cultural or social relevancy as is debated in many quarters of the church. This book is not about how worship services should be structured or how messages should be prepared and delivered. This book does not claim to have all the answers as to the relevancy of the church today. The single message of this book is about propelling the church into having greater impact in the world through strategic leadership.

Some within the church content that the problem the church has today is a world that is becoming more secular and humanistic. They argue that any attempt at making the church relevant would dilute the message of the church. While this book does not attempt to get involved into such debate; the simple premise of this book is that everything rises and falls on leadership. The problem of the church is not secularism or humanism. The world has always and will always have a secular worldview. But with strategic leadership, the church can have greater impact, restore its image, and reach a troubling world with the message of hope and grace through our Lord Jesus Christ.

This book is intended to be an encouragement and a resource to the body of Christ on how to make the church more strategic in its approach in making the vision and mission relevant to the world. Chapter 1 discusses strategic management as a need in the local church, not just at the denominational hierarchy level. Chapter 2 is a perspective on the historical development of leadership models and the lessons we can learn to help us make our vision, values, and mission more relevant without diluting our message in a troubling world. In chapter 3, data mining and analysis is discussed as a guide to practical and reasonable strategic planning. Chapter 4 is about the impact of strategic planning in the local church. In chapter 5, the emphasis is on understanding organizational paradigms and adapting to maximize relevancy in a postmodern world. Chapter 6 is about strategy formulations and implementations, and chapter 7 discusses how to develop a winning strategic plan.

It is my prayer and hope that this book will propel the body of Christ no matter the doctrinal persuasion in gaining an advantage in reaching the world with our values and message. It is my aspiration that this brief but concise leadership book will position the church to plan strategically so that we can have maximum impact no matter the scope of our visions and mission.

May the grace of our Lord Jesus Christ enable you as you read this book, and may there be an impartation of the Holy Spirit as you use this book as a resource to plan strategically.

CHAPTER ONE

STRATEGIC MANAGEMENT: A NEED IN THE LOCAL CHURCH

> *Suppose one of you wants to build a tower. Will he not first sit down and estimate the cost to see if he has enough money to complete it? For if he lays the foundation and is not able to finish it, everyone who sees it will ridicule him, saying, "This fellow began to build and was not able to finish." Or suppose a king is about to go to war against another king. Will he not first sit down and consider whether he is able with ten thousand men to oppose the one coming against him with twenty thousand? If he is not able, he will send a delegation while the other is still a long way off and will ask for terms of peace.*
>
> —Luke 14:28–32, NIV

Our lord and master Jesus taught the importance of strategic planning in the above Scripture. Yet many church leaders today are neglecting this important biblical principle to properly plan.

No wonder most of our programs are limited in their scope and cannot produce maximum impact upon our communities. No wonder the church is seemingly less attractive to the world. The American Religion Identification Survey (2008), a research-based study released in 2009 indicated professing Christians in the United States declined from 86 percent in 1990 to 77 percent in 2001. Most research-based studies revealed churches are closing their doors daily in the United States, and many are slowly declining around the world. Olson (2008) in his groundbreaking research of over 200,000 churches declared about 3,707 churches closed their doors between 2000 to 2005. According to the Keep God in America website (2010), 3,500 to 4,000 churches are closed each year in America with a sharp decline in Sunday attendance.

Based upon these alarming statistics, there is a need for strategic leadership within the local church. Strategic leadership as described in this book is not about being knowledgeable, gifted, or talented. Knowledge, gifts, and/or talents are important qualities that may determine the strength and/or weakness of a leader, but they should not be the only means by which the ability to lead is judged. Strategic leadership should not be defined in term of charisma. We have learned from history that great leaders can either be "charismatic or dull, generous or tightfisted, visionary or number oriented" (Drucker, 2004, p.1). It does not matter how a leader defines him/herself; an effective leader will not fit in a strict jacket. Schaeffer (2002), high-lighting leadership traits, suggests "an autocratic leader sometimes has to be participative, and a reformer some-times needs to act like an autocrat" (p.1). By considering the different roles leaders need to assume at different times, strategic leaders are better able to think through the ways decisions are made. They can create the atmosphere to effectively communicate with people and manage their time in such a way that they are able to address the most pressing needs of the organization at the moment.

Strategic leadership is the ability to exert influence on organizational performance. A strategic leader has the capability to overcome major inertial forces that keep organizations from successfully adapting to new trends. A strategic leader can inspire and motivate stakeholders. The key role of a strategic leader is to create cohesion among the members of the organization with the vision and power to implement strategic change.

Strategic leadership within the local church will force the church to challenge common assumptions and deconstruct perceptions and practices (traditions). We need to understand that if the church must influence society, there is a need for leaders that can force the church to challenge common assumptions held about the role of the church within the community. By challenging common assumptions, the strategic leader can enhance the influence of the local church within the community. In every age, from the preclassical to this postmodern age, strategic leaders had spiked innovations by challenging traditional thought patterns. For example, it was challenging common assumptions and thought patterns that gave birth to the Protestant Reformation. If everyone was contended with the teachings and practices, we would never have Protestantism today.

For a leader to be strategic in his/her approach, that leader must be willing to think critically. Kirby and Goodpaster (2002), suggest that critical thoughts spring from creativity, logical reasoning, analysis, and investigations. Ruggiero (2004), as well as Schwarze and Lape (2001), stress the importance of evaluation, methodical analysis, and objective reasoning as components of critical thinking. In essence, critical thinking involves evaluating information in an analytical manner with the goal of making judgment and conclusions that can lead to innovation as well as challenge common assumptions.

Keep in mind that a critical thinker does not just gather information. That which distinguishes a critical thinker from all others is the ability to focus on information in a way that stimulates deep probing. In fact, critical thinking can be classified as the outcome of deep inquiries coupled with careful analysis and evaluation of facts (Ruggiero 2004). The critical thinker gathers information in an organized and methodical manner, and then analyzes the information within the context of creativity, objectivity, using at times an investigative approach with the goal of reaching conclusions that can lead to stimulative dialogue.

It is time we realize that leadership should not be known or recognized by personality but by the questions a leader asks in fulfilling his/her purpose. The questions a leader asks help him/her to understand what needs to be done, and what is fight for the organization. The questions also enable the leader to develop action plans, take responsibility for decisions, take responsibility for communication, focus on opportunities rather than problems, run productive meetings, and have a mindset of a team player (Drucker 2004). In other words, what makes an individual effective leader is the fact that the person seeks out information or knowledge needed for strategic planning. The leader then converts such knowledge into action and strategically interact with all stakeholders to ensure that the whole organization feels responsible and accountable. Strategic leaders always ask probing questions and look at the pros and cons, advantages, and disadvantages, facts and assumptions surrounding an issue before formulating an opinion. By critically examining assumptions, the strategic leader can avoid situations that most often could exist in the realm of doubt. Kirby and Goodpaster (2002) suggest, "The extent to which you are able to think critically about ideas that conflict with your basic attitudes and values is inversely related to the extent to which you are enculturated" (p. 14). For example, I am more comfortable as a Pentecostal believer and can readily defend my faith not because of dogma but based on Scriptural and historical facts that are not easily refutable. Growing up in conservative Pentecostal Christian family, I always went outside of my circle of faith and listened to the opposing views of non-Pentecostal Christians. When I accepted the call to ministry, I enrolled at a non-Pentecostal (very anti-Pentecostal) Calvinistic theological school. Although I did not understand strategic leadership at that time and did not see myself as a strategic leader then, I chose an anti-Pentecostal school because I needed to understand why some believers believe as they do. This approach led me to do a background, historical, and cultural investigative studies about the differences in what I was taught within my circle and that which was taught outside of my circle. The more I investigated, the better my understanding of what led to the conflicting views and vast disagreement and diversity within the Christian faith. Now my Pentecostal heritage is unshakable than it would have been if only based on dogma.

We are emotional being (logical thinking) and are affected positively or negatively by the emotions we feel at a particular time. Yet when it comes to critical thinking, we cannot allow our emotions or feelings to cloud our objectivity. It should become the responsibility of the strategic leader to accept critique and feedback in a manner that promotes and encourages a more collaborative approach. While most leaders may have the knowledge of what to do to shape the focus and scope of the organization, a strategic leader does not always put his personal agenda ahead. Instead, the leader asks other leaders and stakeholders what ought to be done at the time. This strengthens the position of the leader as a strategic planner and partner. Asking what needs to be done now can lead to many suggestions and tasks that could stretch any leader in many directions. But the task of a strategic leader is to sift through the many suggested tasks, sets priorities, and sticks to them.

Strategic leadership pays close attention to details as this enables the effective communication of opportunities and strategic decision making. For example, if a decision has been made, who are the ones responsible for its implementation? Is there a deadline and who are those affected the most by the decision? Are they properly informed, and do they clearly understand the decision to the point that they will not strongly oppose it? Have the objectives of the decision being clearly communicated so as to strengthen partnership and implementation? We need to realize that "leadership is not a state, it's a journey" (Schaeffer 2002, p.1). To succeed it is important to make the necessary adjustment that will strengthen endeavors and improve efficiency. It is my prayer and hope that church leaders take a closer look at Jesus's statement, "For the children of this world are in their generation wiser than the children of light" (Luke 16:8, KJV), and make the necessary adjustment to strengthen our endeavors in proclaiming the message of God's grace through Jesus to a lost world.

Denominationalism and Strategic Leadership in the Local Church

Stetzer (2010), made an interesting observation that as churches decline, the local pastor is stressed out and "become more concerned about a well-used policy manual than a well-used baptistery" (par. 3). Because it takes more than personality and skills to succeed as a leader, local pastors are more successful in organizations with a strong support system. Michael Allison (2002), suggests that some leaders are less successful in one organization than others because of the lack of what he terms structured assistance (p. 350). He further implies that it is difficult for any leader to be effective if the board cannot "support independence and strength (as opposed to dependency and compliance) in their board leadership" (p. 350). He supports his theory by stating that, "No matter how hard [a leader] tries, one individual cannot ensure a safe future for the organization he or she has worked so hard to lead and build" (p. 351).

It would not be enough to talk about strategic leadership within the local church without speaking about the role of the denominational hierarchy as it relates to the local leadership. While most denominational leaders I spoke with claimed they do not unnecessarily interfere with the local churches, the policies and practices at times make it difficult for the local pastor to break forth with innovation. Although many churches are autonomous within some denominational circles, the local pastor is often held back by the constitution and the board of trustee.

Denominational leaders need to realize that organizational effectiveness starts at the local level and is essential for direction and proficiency. When an organization loses its effectiveness because of undue control and a lack of strong support through unhealthy practices, it becomes difficult to easily identify the proper or right thing to do. A lack of support for the vision of the local pastor, be it the local church's constitution and/or the unwillingness to change practices by the board of trustee, can create a deficit in organizational effectiveness because it acts as a brake on the local pastor's creativity and innovation.

Denominational leaders can remove the deficit brake off the local pastor by seeking to improve coordination and corporation by "raising the level of human conduct and ethical aspiration of both the leader and the led" (Banerji and Krishnan 2000, p. 405). This can be done by rallying each leader within the local church and the entire membership around the vision of the local pastor. Another way of removing the deficit brake off the local pastor is for the denominational leadership to carefully consider the potentials of the local pastor and the congregation and then mentor and coach the pastor with the goal of bringing out the best in the pastor and the leadership team.

No denomination can claim growth without growth within the local churches. Problems at the local church level can affect the image and effectiveness of the denomination. Therefore, the focus and emphasis of regional or district leaders should not be control or power but motivating the local pastors to positively contribute to the process of growth. By motivating the local pastor to become a strategic planner and supporting a corporative atmosphere within the local church, there can be a real influence in relationship among the leaders, leading to real changes that reflect their mutual purposes.

It is my opinion that the role of the denominational hierarchy should be providing meaning and value, not unduly controlling processes at the local church level. Meaning and values are essential to the development and sustenance of organizational culture. By creating meanings, organizations can help shape the perspectives of all stakeholders. By creating an atmosphere of shared values, organizations can influence the behaviors of stakeholders. Creating meaning is of essence to any organization. Denominational leaders need to realize that creating meaning can position the local church into aligning the mission objectives with the strategic objective in a way that propels the local church into having an advantage within the community.

What Does It Mean to Create Meaning?

There are multiple assumptions that are underlying factors in decision making. Even with the collection and interpretation of data (discussed in chapter 3), organizations have assumptions that affect why and how data are collected and interpreted. The challenge then is for leaders to examine those assumptions in a proactive manner thereby enhancing the capacity of the organization to cope with changing trends in a continuously changing environment. This is where denominational leadership should be supportive of the local church leadership.

Creating meaning as it relates to strategic leadership within the local church is providing clarity by challenging common assumptions that affect the decision-making process. The clarity can be best provided by the denominational leadership as a mean of enhancing the vision of the local pastor. The first step to providing meaning in the local church is to clarify the language of legal documents. As suggested by Sarup (1993), language has different meaning and the strategic leader must continuously bring to the forefront the "the discrepancy between meaning and the author's assertion" (p. 52). Most of the legal documents like the local church's constitution and/or the policy and procedures manuals of the denomination have languages that must be constantly clarify to avoid creating a situation that can affect the influence and impact of the local church. According to Zabel (2004), creating meaning focuses on "fostering active thinking or problem solving" (p. 6). In other word, creating meaning helps the denominational and local church leaderships to effectively understand the past and adapt so as to meet their strategic objectives. Creating meaning can help both the denominational and local church leadership synthesize and give perspective to the vast volume of information available on every subject matter.

For example, I was surprised during my research that some church constitutions have age restriction for the lead pastor. To create meaning, the strategic leader needs to ask and seek to understand why the age restriction? Let's look at a real situation (although I will not name the local church or denomination) in which meaning needs to be created if the local church must survive. The church's constitution states that the lead pastor must be at least thirty-five years old. The church has an aging congregation and wants to attract young people but has limited financial capacity to hire a youth pastor. The church does not have a pastor as the founding pastor is aged and currently in an assisted living facility. They bring in guest pastors that are over sixty years old each Sunday. The church currently has a twenty-three years old Bible college student, but he is not qualified according to the constitution to be the lead pastor. The church is declining in membership, has no impact in the community, and is on the verge of closing down. Everything is run by a board of trustee that has all members over 55 years old. If this church must survive, the denominational leadership much create meaning to the language of the constitution. The first step is to seek to understand the rationale behind the age restriction. The next step would be to look at current trend within that local church and ask whether the age restriction is still necessary for a small and aging congregation that has a potential youthful pastor and a church that needs to attract young people to continue to be relevant within the community.

Let's look at another scenario that is affecting another congregation I surveyed. The constitution states that women cannot exert authority over men but did not say women cannot become pastor for a local congregation. For the past ten years, the congregation has gone through six pastors with none having any impact within the church or the community. However, there is a woman with a notable call into ministry who has kept everything in order. Without her leadership, there would be no congregation. Yet the language of the constitution seems to forbid her from officially leading the church. Membership has sharply declined with each new pastor. A congregation of about 120 people ten years ago is now a congregation of 55 aging people. Unless the language of the constitution is clarified, this local church could close down when there is a strong woman that could bring life to this congregation and impact the community for Christ.

Another interesting situation I came across is a church in a suburb that is dying because of a common assumption (not a written document) that only white males should lead. There has been a shift in demography some years now. The once all-white community is now diverse. Current population is about 36 percent white, 32 percent black, 20 percent Hispanic, and 12 percent other ethnicity. The white pastor of this church is now sixty-eight years old and wants to retire but cannot find another white pastor to replace him. The church has three black pastors and two Hispanic pastors all serving in various capacities on a volunteer basis. But this local congregation with such potential for growth is declining because of an assumption that Black and Hispanic cannot serve as lead pastor in a so-called diverse congregation. Unless meaning is created, there exists a potential for split and the end of what could be a unique congregation in an already segregated church atmosphere in most churches in America.

McKernon (2002), suggests that creating meaning is "explaining how the world changes, how we explain it, and how we deal with it day-to-day" (p. 10). In the examples cited above, those churches still have the chance to survive. All stakeholders need to understand and accept the changing trends as well as learn to deal with the trends in a proactive manner. Leaders need to understand that people will most likely choose practices and make decisions based upon their beliefs and values. By creating meaning, the strategic leader can help synthesize and give perspective. By creating meaning, organizations and individuals can be empowered to cope effectively with the challenges of a changing world. Besides decision making, creating meaning can lead to values that can help shape the behavior of all stakeholders within an organization. Organizational values can ensure that all stakeholders relate to each other in a way that promotes a commitment to teamwork for higher productivity, efficiency, and professionalism in all that is done in the name of the organization. Shared values can create an atmosphere of commitment and can also influence behaviors in the areas of integrity, truthfulness, authenticity, and a commitment to treat one another with respect and dignity. By creating meaning, strategic leadership at all levels of the church can address "new situations or negotiate [with] complex institutions" (Mika et al. 2005, p. 351) about issues that are necessary for their mission and critical success factors.

The Apostle Paul is a classic example of a strategic leader who synthesized and gave perspective to the volume of information that was available to him. William Barclay (1970), portrayed Paul as a strategic leader who created meaning in his messages. Creating meaning is about the manner in which we organize knowledge and use the information to enhance flexibility in the application process. Speaking about the manner in which the Apostle Paul used information, Barclay (1970) states, "In his missionary approach Paul had no set scheme and formula; his approach was completely flexible. He began where his audience was" (p. 166).

To clarify this point, let us look at three of the sermons of the Apostle Paul as highlighted by Barclay (1970) from the book of Acts of the Apostles in the New Testament: the sermon preached in the synagogue in Antioch in Pisidia (Acts 13:16–41), the sermon preached in Athens (Acts 17:22–31), and the sermon preached in Lystra (Acts 14:15–17).

Paul's message in Antioch, Pisidia, was in a synagogue to Jews, to proselytes, and to Godfearers (Acts 13:16–41).

a. Paul therefore began in Jewish history and used the Old Testament as an arsenal of proof texts to prove his case (vs. 16–23).

And Paul, getting up and making a sign with his hand, said, Men of Israel, and you who have the fear of God, give ear. The God of this people Israel made selection of our fathers, lifting the people up from their low condition when they were living in the land of Egypt, and with a strong arm took them out of it. And for about forty years he put up with their ways in the waste land. And hav-ing put to destruction seven nations in the land of Canaan, he gave them the land for their heritage for about four hundred and fifty years. And after these things he gave them judges, till the time of Samuel the prophet. Then at their request for a king, God gave them Saul, the son of Kish, a man of the family of Benjamin, who was their king for forty years. And having put him on one side, he made David their king, to whom he gave witness, saying, I have taken David, the son of Jesse, a man dear to my heart, who will do all my pleasure.

> From this man's seed has God given to Israel a Saviour, even Jesus, as he gave his word. (BBE)

b. Paul moved onto the immediate preparation for Jesus by John the Baptist (verses 24, 25).

> For whose coming John made ready the way by preaching to all the people of Israel the baptism which goes with a change of heart. And when John was completing his work, he said, what do I seem to you to be? I am not he; but one is coming after me, whose shoes I am not good enough to undo. (BBE)

c. Paul proceeded to the narrative of Jesus's rejection, death, and resurrection (verses 26–31).

> My brothers, children of the family of Abraham, and those among you who have the fear of God, to us the word of this salvation is sent. For the men of Jerusalem and their rulers, having no knowledge of him, or of the sayings of the prophets which come to their ears every Sabbath day, gave effect to them by judging him. And though no cause of death was seen in him, they made a request to Pilate that he might be put to death. And when they had done all the things said in the Writings about him, they took him down from the tree, and put him in the place of the dead. But God gave him back from the dead: And for a number of days he was seen by those who came with him from Galilee to Jerusalem, who are now his witnesses before the people. (BBE)

d. Paul claimed that all these events were foretold in prophecy (verses 32–39) and quotes the appropriate prophecies.

> And we are giving you the good news of the undertaking made to the fathers, Which God has now put into effect for our children, by sending Jesus; as it says in the second Psalm, You are my Son; this day I have given you being. And about his coming back from the dead, never again to go to destruction, he has said these words, I will give you the holy and certain mercies of David. Because he says in another Psalm, You will not let your Holy One see destruction. Now David, having done God's work for his generation, went to sleep, and was put with his fathers, and his body came to destruction: But he, who was lifted up by God, did not see destruction. And so, let it be clear to you, my brothers, that through this man forgiveness of sins is offered to you: And through him everyone who has faith is made free from all those things, from which the law of Moses was not able to make you free. (BBE)

e. Paul concluded with a warning to those who still reject the offer of God in Jesus Christ (verses 40, 41).

> So take care that these words of the prophets do not come true for you; See, you doubters, have wonder and come to your end; for I will do a thing in your days to which you will not give belief, even if it is made clear to you. (BBE)

Since Paul's audience was deeply rooted in Jewish history and in the scriptures, his "preaching was not take-it-or-leave-it proclamation" (Barclay 1970, p.166). "It was proclamation plus explanation and defense. The characteristic word of Paul's preaching in the synagogue is the word *argued*. In Damascus, in Thessalonica, in Athens, in Corinth, in Ephesus Paul argued in the synagogue (Acts 9:22; 17:2, 17; 18:4; 19: 8). The faith was proclaimed and defended at the same time. Acceptance of it was not given on a wave of emotion; from the beginning the mind had to be satisfied as well as the heart" (p. 166).

In Athens, Paul began from local religious worship (Acts 17:23–28), and he quoted from the Greek poets (Acts 17:28).

a. Paul started with the history of the search of the soul for God (Acts 17:23–28).

    For as I walked around and looked carefully at your objects of worship, I even found an altar with this inscription: TO AN UNKNOWN GOD. Now what you worship as something unknown I am going to proclaim to you. "The G od w ho made the world and everything in it is the Lord of heaven and earth and does not live in temples built by hands. And he is not served by human hands, as if he needed anything, because he him-self gives all men life and breath and everything else. From one man he made every nation of men that they should inhabit the whole earth; and he determined the times set for them and the exact places where they should live. God did this so that men would seek him and perhaps reach out for him and find him, though he is not far from each one of us. "For in him we live and move and have our being." As some of your own poets have said, "We are his offspring." (NIV)

Barclay (1970) points out that Paul never mentions Jewish history, and he makes no quotation from the scriptures. He knew that it would be futile to talk about a history which no one knew and to quote from a book which no one had read and the authority of which no one would accept.

b. Paul presented the coming of Jesus Christ as God's decisive event, stating, "The times of ignorance God overlooked, but now he commands all men everywhere to repent" (verse 30).

c. Paul proclaimed the fact of the resurrection and the threat of judgment (verse 31).

In Lystra (Acts 14:15–17), Paul "was out in the wilds. Certainly no one there would know any-thing about Jewish history or Jewish scriptures. Lystra had not the widely disseminated culture of Athens, and there was no point in quoting the Greek poets" (Barclay 1970, 167).

a. Paul started straight from nature, from the sun and the wind and the rain and the growing things stressing the continuing activity of God (verses 15, 17).

Men, why are you doing this? We too are only men, human like you. We are bringing you good news, telling you to turn from these worthless things to the living God, who made heaven and earth and sea and everything in them…Yet he has not left himself without testimony: He has shown kindness by giving you rain from heaven and crops in their seasons; he provides you with plenty of food and fills your hearts with joy. (NIV)

b. The Apostle Paul stressed the mercy and grace of God toward all mankind, stating, "In past generations he (God) allowed all the nations to walk in their own ways" (Acts 14:16).

It's about time the local church embraces strategic leadership so as to give us an advantage in reaching the world with the message of the grace and love of God at their levels as the Apostle Paul did. As we create meaning and enhance our values, it's time we take into account the whole and not just the part. It's about time we shift our focus from looking at an individual as the only source of authority. If the local church must experience growing impact within the community, overdependence on hierarchical authority must be minimized. What we need to encourage is a healthy interpersonal relationship at all levels. The emphasis should be on change, empowerment, collaboration, people and relationships, diversity, and the proper sharing and utilization of knowledge in this information age.

CHAPTER TWO

A PERSPECTIVE ON THE HISTORICAL DEVELOPMENT OF LEADERSHIP MODELS

Leadership is very crucial to organization's success. In its simplicity, leadership is positively influencing others to action. Yet leadership over the years has had different connotations and meant different things to different people. This chapter gives a perspective on the historical development of leadership models over the years. The goal of the historical perspective is to help the body of Christ realize that leadership is not stagnant and that changing trends requires innovation to be relevant.

A Historical Overview of the Leadership Models

It is necessary as we discuss the need for strategic leadership within the local church to briefly look at the historical development of leadership models.

As Wren (2004) states, "a study of the past contributes to a more logical, coherent picture of the present. Without a knowledge of history, individuals have only their own limited experiences as a basis for thought and action" (p.6).

Preclassical Era Leadership Model

This era started with an emphasis on *institutionalization with centralized authority*. Proponents of this view were Nicolo Machiavelli and Thomas Hobbes. Machiavelli advocated that centralization of authority would effectively deal with the inherent evil nature within man. Hobbes, on the other hand, stressed the absolute power of the centralized leadership and the complete obedience of the subjects as a means of bringing order and eliminating anarchy (Wren 2004). The goal of centralized institutions as taught by Machiavelli and Hobbes was to enable the leadership to focus on the need to have "specify policies, procedures…and authority" (p. 22).

However, as the society began to advocate for change with the emerging of other religious sects, coupled with the desire for separation of power between religions and state, three ideologies emerged, bringing some forms of order to the new society that was replacing the old order. Those leadership ideologies are known as the Protestant ethic, liberty ethic, and market ethic (Wren 2004).

The Protestant ethic "was a challenge to the central authority of the church and a response to the needs of the people for achievement" (Wren 2004, 67). Weber argued that the leadership alternative offered by the Protestant led to Capitalism (Wren 2004). The Protestant emphasized that every "occupation was a calling, and all were legitimate in the sight of God" (p. 38). Protestantism taught that "to attain self-confidence, people had to engage in intense worldly activity [like business], for that and that alone could dispel religious doubts and give certainty of grace" (p. 38).

The liberty ethic "sought to protect individual rights" (Wren 2004, p. 67). The emphasis was on ensuring that those in authority do not abuse the basis rights of the individual. People need to be treated equally, respectfully, and not deprive of essential justice as a means of promoting a healthy relationship and motivating better productivity. A strong proponent of human rights during this era was John Locke. He pioneered the idea that the led should be able to judge the conducts of the leader as a means of ensuring that the basis rights of the followers are not violated by the leaders.

The market ethic advocated for the formulation of a system of leadership with decentralized authority to enable local leaders effectively deal with issues within their jurisdictions. The goal of the market ethic was to ensure that power is decentralized as a means of stopping abuse.

Classical Era Leadership Model

The classical era was a time of industrialization. Inventions led to the building of factories to speed up production as compared to that which was done manually either by man or animal. With the factories came the need for more workers. People had to put aside their family businesses and farmlands and worked in the factories for better income. The factories with their larger workforce created the need for a leadership model that could both achieve and sustain the desired goal of each factory and the needs of the people. Wren (2004) describes the challenge of this era as followed:

> The emerging factory system posed management problems different from those ever encountered before. The church could organize and manage its properties because

> of dogma and the devotion of the faithful; the military could control large numbers of personnel through rigid hierarchy of discipline and authority; and governmental bureaucracies could operate without having to meet competition or show a profit. The managers in the new factory system could not resort to any of these devices to ensure the proper utilization of resources. (p. 15)

The many factories created an environment of competition during this era. Yet the factory system lacked effective leadership in a market environment that was becoming very competitive with a large number of unskilled laborers. Coupled with this managerial lack was the issue of the lack of motivation, leading to underproduction. The goal was to ensure that laborers were motivated, trained, and treated ethically. Another problem was that most of the laborers had not adjusted well to the rigid routines of the factory system. There was a need for a leadership model that could motivate laborers and earn the trust of these workers, thereby gaining their loyalty and commitment.

To address these leadership challenges, an incentive-focused model was developed. Wren (2004) described the leadership model as "positive inducements (the carrot), negative sanctions (the stick), and…methods for providing motivation and discipline" (p. 25). The focus of this leadership model was motivation. The emphasis was on paying workers based upon their individual levels of production. In other words, the better the output, the better the wages. This incentives focused leadership model was advanced by Adam Smith. Breaking away from the prevailing view that the "worker must be kept at the subsistence level and that the best worker was the hungriest one" (p. 28), Smith advocated that "monetary incentives brought out the best in people and that they would work harder to get more" (p. 28). Monetary incentives were not just in the form of increment in wages. Laborers were paid their regular wages while learning, especially if it related to improved attitudes and input on the job. However, while monetary incentives were been offered for better outputs, punishments were meted out on those who were negligent to duty by with-holding their money in the form of fines.

Modernism Leadership Model

The modern era saw great advancement in science and technology. As a result, most of the jobs were mechanical in nature, like railroad constructions with many working in the steel industry.

The skills required to operate machineries coupled with a large workforce created a scarcity of jobs. The outcome of this job scarcity led to workers limited their outputs as a means of job security. Laborers felt that working faster and maximizing output would result in the lack of job since the specific task would be completed, and they would have to wait for another project to get an income.

Frederick Taylor, who worked his way from common laborer to chief engineer in six years with Midvale Steel in Philadelphia and served with the company for twelve years, from 1878 to 1890, offered the first solution to the managerial challenge of the modern era known as scientific management (Wren 2004). Taylor based his scientific management theory on his analysis of the problem which he described as "bad industrial conditions, [with] worker restriction of output, poor management, and lack of harmony between workers and managers" (p. 318). He blamed management for these problems because laborers were paid hourly wages with no monetary incentives for hard work. In Taylor's mind, management created an atmosphere of slothfulness by eliminating the monetary incentive reward system for hard work. The scientific management model as proposed by Taylor and improved upon by many required that "management should have the responsibility for setting standard, planning work, and devising incentive schemes" (Wren 2004, p. 322).

Another person who affected managerial practices during this era was Henri Fayol. He advanced the idea of focusing more on managerial functions than technical skills. He proposed the need for strategic planning, making of budgetary allocations, division of labor, and order and structure for smooth operation (Wren 2004).

Postmodernism Leadership Model

Postmodernism is characterized by participative and transformational leadership. Postmodernism emphasizes leadership models like the charismatic, participative, transactional, transformational, and innovation. Postmodernists encourage enhancing performance through a healthy interpersonal relationship by encouraging full participation, which strengthens morale and motivates others to progressive action. However, it appears that the most desired model is the transformational (Wren 2004). Transformational leadership encourages full participation and enhances performance through a healthy interpersonal relationship that strengthens morale and motivates others to progressive action. The focus and emphasis of transformational leadership is not control or power but getting others motivated to positively contribute to the process. Lawlor (2006) states that, "Transformational leadership is not confined to the organizational hierarchy, as it courageously and politically empowers others into the role of leadership" (par. 11).

Wren (2004), suggests the more people searched for answers to the essence and nature of leadership, the more theorists and organizations realized it is best to move away from the autocratic style with its emphasis on inherited or family traits. Weiskittel (1999), suggests at the turn of the nineteenth century, the emphasis started to shift from personal to group interest. Theorists began to focus more on fostering a sense of belonging. As we moved into the twentieth century, participation through motivation began the concern of a lot of theorists. The focus was now on the rational, traditional, and charismatic classifications of leadership. To many, motivating others to action and ownership through full participation could bring forth transformation in any organization (Harrison 1999). Thus, the transformational theory was embraced. The goal was to influence relationship among leaders and their collaborators, who intend real changes that reflect their mutual purposes.

Philosophy and Organizational Development

Over the years, many organizations had incorporated philosophical principles to help them make decisions that are believed to enhance organizational development and improve relations with employees, customers, and other stakeholders. Philosophy is intended to aid in the understanding of the nature, classifications, and purposes of knowledge. The primary purpose of knowledge is to enhance the process of decision making that leads to actions. From the preclassical to the modern eras, many models and theories were developed. Some of those models and theories are briefly discussed below.

Traditional/Conventional Models Embodied in Philosophy

Management theorists used the philosophical principle of asking probing questions to help their understanding of challenges faced by organizations. The goal of using probing question was to aid the theorists in the process of seeking "accurate information" (Goldman 1999, p. 4). The most common probing questions asked were, "What's best? What's next? What if...? [and] What's my best bet? [These questions are intended to ensure] optimization, forecasting, modeling, simulation, and decision analysis" (Whalen & Samaddar, 2001, p. 292). Out of these questions, some of the most successful traditional models like linear and nonlinear programming, time series and causal regression models, "what if" simulation analysis, and decision trees were developed.

Leadership attitudes and actions regarding organizational development were centered on using either or a combination of the models (linear and nonlinear programming, time series and causal regression models, "what if" simulation analysis, and decision trees) to seek out the cause of the problem in a precise manner and utilize the right method or tool needed to solve the problem. As for the relationship with employees, customers, and other stakeholders, the attitudes and actions of leaders were geared toward motivating employees through incentive-based packages as a means of gaining their loyalty and commitment.

Traditional/Conventional Theories Embodied in Philosophy

Philosophers emphasize knowledge can be gained through reasoning, observation, experience, interaction, and our concept of truth (Moser & VanderNat, 2002). Management theorists build upon the philosophical principles of gaining knowledge through reasoning and interaction to develop theories that are believed to enhance organizational behavior and development. The theories are based upon either a "criterion or test of truth…the theory of evidence, justification, or truth determination [with the goal being helping organizations to determine] when it is appropriate to accept a proposition as true, or how to go about determining the truth or falsity of a proposition" (Goldman, 1999, p. 41). Some of the philosophical theories are pragmatism, verificationism, consensus consequentialism, and proceduralism.

Pragmatism focuses on the impact a person's values or beliefs might have on the decisions made. In other words, people will most often choose practices and make decisions based upon their beliefs and values. Therefore, it is important that "whatever people intrinsically value, choosing the best practices that conduce to those values requires true belief " (Goldman 1999, p. 75). Verificationism requires every proposition to be justified by evidence. Consensus consequentialism focuses on creating an atmosphere of collaboration through consensus building. Proceduralism focuses on the processes used to strategize and move the organization forward (Goldman, 1999). Benhabib (1992) is quoted by Goldman (1999) as saying that proceduralism requires "each participant must have an equal chance to initiate and to continue communication; each must have an equal chance to make assertions, recommendations, and explanations; all must have equal chances to express their wishes, desires, and feelings" (p. 77).

Based upon these theories, management theorists have developed the following practices to help leadership attitudes and actions regarding organizational development and relations with employees, customers, and other stakeholders. The practices focused on applying special skills as a means of deriving solutions to the challenges faced by organizations.

Whalen and Samaddar (2001), suggest the practices are used to bridge the "gap between what is perceived and what is desired...[in an attempt to find] an opportunity or ambition to raise the organization's performance to new heights or to achieve improvement by exploiting new methods or new areas of operation" (p. 293). One such practice is the "mating of a problem to a puzzle to form a model that can be solved" (p. 292). The skills used in this practice "range from algorithms that are deterministic and guaranteed to succeed if given enough time, to heuristics and hunches that are fallible but offer impressive savings in time and effort when they succeed" (p. 293). Other practices are forecasting problems using assumptions, creating a formula for predicting data, and using analogy to analyze problems and derive decisions (Whalen & Samaddar, 2001).

Through the use of these practices, leaders can develop critical thinking skills by asking probing questions that challenge the underlying assumptions that created the problem. By critically thinking through the problem, leaders can seek out alternatives solutions. By carefully considering alternative actions, leadership can transform and expand the organization through the "use of flowcharts, checklists, and menus to help humans through complex procedures" (p. 296).

Culture and Organizational Development

Every culture is unique, but with the emphasis on globalization, organizations are expected to use best practices that adhere to ethical standards and promote diversity and a healthy interpersonal relationship. From the preclassical era to postmodernism, cultures have evolved. As cultures changed, so have the models, theories, and practices people draw on to create a realistic, objective picture of the world.

Traditional/Conventional Models Embodied in Culture

Despite the diversity in culture, almost every culture is dealing with the issues of changing trends in labor, ethical trade, upholding basis human rights, and monetary incentives for a cohesive and collaborative workforce. More importantly, the focus is on developing a mentoring and coaching relationship with the goal of making the mentees proficient and productive workers. The emphasis is not about control or power but getting others motivated to positively contribute to the process.

With such challenges and the emphasis on globalization, management theorists often seek "fixed, stable, unified, comprehensive, structured, universally-applicable truths and an objective knowledge of consuming and marketing" (McKernon, 2002, para.13). Every models, theories, and practice is intended to "explain the world by decontextualizing and reducing complexity or change to relatively simple facts and formulae" (McKernon 2002, para. 13).

Reflection

Each of the leadership models and philosophies discussed were effective during their time although they were all initially resisted. The models and philosophies helped leaders to understand the "what and why" of the prevailing need of the time. More importantly, the models helped leaders and mangers to align the "what and why" of the organization with the "how and when," thereby enabling society and organizations to better cope with changing trends. Study of these models can help us as the body of Christ understand the fundamentals of leadership and management, as well as create an atmosphere for leaders within the local churches to understand the importance of organizational culture adapting to trends of the time so as to strategize for maximum impact.

Coping with change is never an easy task and requires planning and possible adaptation to changing trends on the part of leadership. The ability of a leader to influence others to achieve a common goal may depend largely on the leadership style employed. Without good leadership substantial progress is difficult if not impossible. Nevertheless, that which may be considered good leadership during an era might not be effective in another time. What is needed then is for those in leadership to modify their approach as a means of rallying others into achieving the goals and objectives of the organization.

Lessons We Can Learn from the Historical Perspective on Leadership Models

The primary lesson we can learn from this historical perspective is the old adage that everything rises and falls on leadership. When leaders are proactive, they cannot be easily swept away by the wave of changing trends in society. For an organization to be relevant, leadership must adapt practices without compromising values. This is why strategic leadership must be embraced by the church. Remember, strategic leadership is the ability to exert influence on organizational performance. A strategic leader has the capability to overcome major inertial forces that keep organizations from successfully adapting to new trends. A strategic leader can inspire and motivate stakeholders. The key role of a strategic leader is to create cohesion among the members of the organization with the vision and power to implement strategic change.

The preclassical era with its emphasis on centralized-institutionalized power was forced to adapt a new approach to leadership as the society changed coupled with the desire for separation of power between religion and state. To cope with the changes in society, leadership was forced to decentralize authority within the workplace. The classical era experienced an environment of competition due to the rise of the factory system. Coping with competition and substantial growth require effective leadership. To sustain growth in the midst of competition, factories had to move toward a more incentive-based approach of leadership. The modern era with its advancement in science and technology had to embrace harmony between workers and managers for maximum output. The need for harmony and maximum output gave rise to bargaining negotiations, which we know as labor unions.

Can the church be relevant in a changing world? I strongly believe we can stop the rapid decline in church attendance and growth by considering the statement of our Lord that, "The children of this world are in their generation wiser than the children of light" (Luke 16:8, KJV). We can be wiser by using our God-given creative insights to influence this generation with the gospel of the grace of God through our Lord Jesus Christ. Our challenge is not secularism or humanism but the lack of strategic leadership. The world has always had secularist and humanist, but the church has prevailed through good leadership and outreach strategies. Our problem is lack of foresight. As Stetzer (2010) suggests, the church at one point in any age has started "strong or experience periods of growth, but then they stagnate. Patterns and traditions that once seemed special eventually lose their meaning. Churches that were once outwardly-focused eventually become worried about the wrong things" (par. 3).

Instead of worrying over the wrong things, local pastors need to influence their congregations to action. Difficult issues should be handled by creating a sense of purpose and ownership. The pastor should have a vision for the local church that is aligned with the mission of the denomination. The vision should be presented to the congregation in an appealing manner to both inspire and motivate the people. The pastor should not be afraid to raise questions that will challenge assumptions, traditions, and beliefs. The pastor should see other leaders in the local church as strategic partners.

Leadership is coping with change through planning and possible adaptation to changing trends as a means of influencing others to become efficient. Yet what many claim about themselves often does not align with their practices. Thus, it is important that in other to bridge the gap between theory and practice, leaders should often deconstruct their leadership assumptions, models, theories, and practices. The deconstruction will help a leader analyze the relevance between what is a claimed and practical reality. The process will also enable the leader to explore alternatives as a means of bridging the gap between what is claimed and that which is practiced. In other words, is there relevance between what a leader claims about himself and practical realities? If not, are there alternatives that can be explored to help the leader bridge the gap between what is claimed and practical realities? Leaders often make claims that are based upon perceptions that are not validated by strong evidence. For example, a person might perceive himself as a transformational leader, thereby assuming that in practice that is the case. When tested by reality, that same person could display traits that are not compatible to transformational leadership.

Definition of Deconstruction

Deconstruction is the process by which differentiations are made between what is claimed and that which is delivered. By differentiating between claims and deliveries, relevance can be derived (Phillips, 2004). To enable any leader unbiasly see relevance between what is claimed as style and what is practiced, it would be best practice to periodically analyze the disparity that exists between espoused theories and practical reality.

Deconstruction is the means by which we critically analyze assumptions we hold about ourselves. This process of analysis helps us identify alternatives that improve our understanding of the claims we make of ourselves (King, 2005).

For example, a person could view himself/herself as a leader that influences others to proactive action that leads to innovation and proficiency. Another person could view himself as a leader that motivates others to take ownership as a means of enhancing productivity. Yet still, another person could perceive himself as a leader that partners with others through collaboration.

Deconstructing Leadership as Influence

Is there relevance between what you as a leader claims about influencing others to become innovative and proficient? If not, are there alternatives that can be explored to help you, as a leader, bridge the gap between what is claimed and practical realities? Do you, as a leader, have the ability to influence others to achieve a common goal? By action, have you, as a leader, created the atmosphere to be trusted? Can others say without hesitation that you, as a leader, have influenced your people to handle difficult issues, thereby creating a sense of purpose within the local church and community? If the answers to these questions are yes, then in the area of influence, the deconstruction shows that what is claimed aligns with practice. If the answers are no, there is a need to seek out alternate styles of leadership that can bridge the gap between what you assume about yourself as a leader and what is the practical reality.

Deconstructing Leadership as Motivation

Motivation can bring out the best in people. Though motivation can take different forms, the essence is to heighten efficiency by meeting people needs. Do you as a leader who claim to be a motivator have a history of focusing on the needs, aspirations, and abilities of the individual members of the church and community? As a perceived motivator, do you easily cope with change through planning and possible adaptation to changing trends? Do you as a leader have in place an incentive plan and package to motivate staffs? Depending on the answer, you can tell if your perception is in alignment with your practices.

Deconstructing Leadership as Partnership

Are you a good collaborator? As a leader, do you always seek out and value inputs from those you lead? Partnership is more than soliciting ideas. As a leader, do you sustain partnership by strongly encouraging and supporting new innovative ideas and methods? While collaborating with others, do you as the leader ensure that interactions with each other is *not* more competitive but collaborative? Based upon this deconstruction, the leader could realize the need to either modify his approach or study how to get staffs, volunteers, and the membership to interact collaboratively.

Conclusion

Organizations need capable decision makers that are knowledgeable to align the strategic objectives with the critical success factors that can give the organization a competitive advantage within the community. Effective decision making within any organization is directly related to the availability of information that can be used to provide insights and clarity to those responsible to make the decision. What I have done in this chapter is to get the right information to those who need it (you, the local church pastor) in an accurate and reliable manner, when the information is needed the most.

Wren (2004), stated "A study of the past contributes to a more logical, coherent picture of the present. Without a knowledge of history, individuals have only their own limited experiences as a basis for thought and action" (p. 6). What is hoped to be achieved in this chapter is to bring pastors and church leaders to a place where we can take a proactive look at ourselves. As leaders, the buck stops with us. If we are willing to cope with changing trends strategically, our congregations and programs will move in the same directions. Grace be multiplied unto you.

CHAPTER THREE

DATA MINING AND ANALYSIS: A GUIDE TO PRACTICAL AND REASONABLE STRATEGIC PLAN

If the local church must be relevant in a postmodern world, leadership should be able to solve problems proactively. Leadership must be willing to learn, understand, and incorporate principles of data mining and analysis into the process of strategic planning. For our purpose here, I will give a brief overview of the importance of data-based problem identification. For those leaders who want to get a grip of data mining and analysis, I would recommend the following authors and books on the subject.

1. Berry, M. J. A. and G. S. Linoff. *Mastering Data Mining.* New York: Wiley, 2000.
2. Edelstein, H. A. *Introduction to Data Mining and Knowledge Discovery* 3rd ed. Potomac, MD: Two Crows Corp, 1999.
3. Fayyad, U. M. et al. *Advances in Knowledge Discovery and Data Mining.* Cambridge, MA: MIT Press, 1996.

4. Fernandez, I., A. Gonzalez, and R. Sabherwal. *Knowledge Management: Challenges, Solutions, and Technologies.* Upper Saddle River, NJ: Prentice-Hall, 2004.
5. Han, J. and M. Kamber. *Data Mining: Concepts and Techniques.* New York: Morgan-Kaufman, 2000.
6. Hastie, T., R. Tibshirani, and J. H. Friedman. *The Elements of Statistical Learning: Data Mining, Inference, and Prediction.* New York: Springer, 2001.
7. Pregibon, D. *Data Mining.* Statistical Computing and Graphics, 7, 8. 1997.
8. Weiss, S. M. and N. Indurkhya. *Predictive Data Mining: A Practical Guide.* New York: Morgan-Kaufman, 1997.
9. Westphal, C. and T. Blaxton. *Data Mining Solutions.* New York: Wiley, 1998.
10. Whalen, T. and S. Samaddar. "Post-Modern Management Science: A Likely Convergence of Soft Computing and Knowledge Management Methods." *Human Systems Management* 20(4) (2001): 291.
11. Witten, I. H. and E. Frank. *Data Mining.* New York: Morgan-Kaufmann, 2000.

Since the focus of this book is strategic planning within the local church, all the details of data mining will not be discussed. The reason we will not discuss the details of data mining is primarily because the process is more useful where huge sum of unrelated data is involved.

The question that might come to mind is why bring up the subject of data mining if you will not discuss the detail of the process. The answer is simple. Many, if not all local churches do not have huge sum of unrelated data to deal with. Some churches don't even think about data collection. What we need to understand as church leaders is that we cannot develop a reasonable and realistic winning strategic plan without some form of data collection, mining, and analysis. The goal of data mining is to establish patterns and predict outcomes.

Scholars suggest that problem identification and interventions are dependent on data collection. Data-based problem identification is an important method because it can "be used to clarify a problem, to establish a baseline, and to measure the efficacy of interventions" (Burns, 2004, p. 64). Data mining is essential to strategic management because data can help with the assessment and diagnosis process. Once the data has been used to properly clarify and analyze the problem, the leadership can effectively explore and select the best interventions.

One major advantage of using data to plan is the fact that proper analysis of the data can aid leaders in selecting the best intervention to whatever problem is foreseen or currently prevailing. More importantly, data mining and analysis make the final outcome of the strategic plan reliable and validated.

A disadvantage would be the misinterpretation and wrong analysis of complex and confusing data thereby leading to faulty intervention that could result in a discredit of the intention of the leadership.

Understanding Data Collection

Data collection as it relates to strategic planning in the local church is simply the gathering of useful information based upon questions that are critical to the success of the church's sustenance and performance. For this reason, when planning to collect data, the question that the strategic leader should ask is how can this church obtain useful information? Keep in mind, data collection is important in helping the organization assess and diagnose patterns of behavior and trends. Data collection should not just be about any information but useful information. When you gather useful information as data, the process of decision making is enhanced. There is assurance the solutions will be more objectives and patterns will be cleared.

For the process of data collection to be effective, the leadership team should establish a data collection plan (DCP). The primary reason for establishing a plan is because more people are involved with the process and they need a guide. For example, the senior pastor would want the data collected within a certain timeline. The data collection plan (DCP) will clearly state the timeline and the prerequisite for the data to be collected. The data collection plan will establish criteria and defined parameters to ensure everyone involved with the process is on the same level.

The data collection plan (DCP) should address the "what," "why," "where," "who," and "how" of the process. The DCP should clearly state why the particular data you want is important. In other words, why does the local church want this data? For example, depending on your situation, you might want to know why your church seems not to be attracting more young people. Or you might want to know why there is no constant dynamic in membership if your membership is always fluctuating. By establishing why you want the data, you will know what information to gather as useful for the process. If you want to improve attendance and membership, financial records of faithful tithe payers could not be useful information unless you want to predict the financial gain if more members are added to the church.

The data collection plan (DCP) should also unambiguously state the purpose of the data. In other words, what will this data do for the local church in her efforts to plan strategically? For example, if the goal is to increase membership, how will the data you plan to gather aid the process? Will the data help the team to understand the culture of the church? Will the data establish behavior pattern in the church? Will the data shed light on the strengths and weaknesses of the discipleship programs? Once you've established the purpose of the data, the leadership team will know exactly where to locate the data.

The next phase in the DCP is where do we locate the specific data. Every data cannot be stored or found in the same place. For example, financial records and new visitors follow-up records could be located within different offices depending on the size and staff of the local church. If you need current mailing list, you need to know where to find the data. If you need listing of families that are no longer coming to church, you need to know exactly where to find that information. Once you've established where to locate the data, you need to clearly state the type of information you want from all the information available in the area you've located to collect your data.

Having established where to locate the data, the next question addressed by the DCP is who should collect which data. Everybody on the team cannot be collecting data randomly. This will lead to confusion and a lack of time management. Specific people should be responsible for specific data. For example, if you want financial data, the person responsible for the financial records should be given the responsibility to collect the specific data needed. If you need to know how many members either moved out of the area or are not coming to church anymore, you need to give the responsibility of collecting the necessary data from whoever has the records. This will save time and remove unnecessary stress on the process. People who have the records and have speedy access can collect the needed information faster than someone who has no clue as to how the information is organized.

By establishing why the data is needed, understanding unambiguously what the data will do, where to locate the data, and who to collect the data, the DCP should conclude with how to collect the right data. When we speak of how to collect the right data, we are simply saying how much data should the team collect? When the data is needed, how available is the information needed? Are there requirements that should be met in obtaining the data? Does the team need special permission from someone other than the senior pastor to collect the data? Should the data be collected in samples, or do we need to review all the information available? Are there costs associated with collecting the data, and how do we cover the cost? These are some of the questions that should be addressed when discussing how to collect the data. Keep in mind the purpose of data collection is to gather useful information that will help the decision making process.

Methods of Data Collection

The methods of data collection are many and varied depending on the specific need and goals of the organization. For our purpose, we will focus on interview and direct observation methods of data collection although basically there are five types of data collection methods.

Interviews are the most common methods of data collections. The purpose of interview "is to obtain the perspectives of key players" (Happ et al. 2004, p. 240). Interview is an excellent way to deep deeper and find solutions to a prevailing problem or situation. Most interviews are done face-to-face with a focus group or individually. To conduct an interview, it is a rule of thumb to obtain a written and/or verbal informed consent prior to the interview.

The leadership can start the process with a topic guide but to encourage more interaction must allow the interview process to be conversational in style so as to enable effective follow up of emerging themes. Interviews can be formal or semistructured and can aid in gathering information that can give a general understanding or a more specific detail of the situation. Questionnaires are often used to foster the process. While interviews can help the exploration of different perceptions about the problem and encourage better participation and inputs into the process, the process is usually time consuming (Davis et al., 2004).

Another method of data collection recommended for the local church as it relates to strategic planning is direct observation. Most often the time and length of the observations primarily "depend on the occurrence or likelihood of the events being studied (Happ et al. 2004, p. 241). Direct observation will do two things for the local church. It will help the leadership team discover and understand the culture of the church and give an understanding as to why certain programs work and some don't achieve the desired results. Observations should be conducted on consecutive days at varying times during the morning, afternoon, and evening when the situations under reviewed are expected to occur. Observations can be done by recording of events. The recording "of event observations can take several forms [like] audio recording, video recording, photograph, semi structured observation tool, or descriptive field note" (Happ et al. 2004, p. 242). For example, your local church has being trying hard to attract young people. You have spent money and time on programs to attract young people, but it seems as though your efforts are not producing the desired results. To solve this problem, you could choose the direct observation method of data collection. You should do the observation on the days and times that the youth group meets. The leadership team can learn patterns and predict the outcomes of the program by means of direct observation. You will learn why the program is not working and what needs to be done to make the program more efficient.

The advantage of using direct observation as a problem identification tool is that it enables the strategic leader to understanding internal interactions as well as the culture including subcultures within the organization and the system operates. A glimpse into the internal networking can give the strategic leader insight into the actual problem. The disadvantage could be that those observed might feel that they are being carefully scrutinized and it might affect their output. The major concerns scholars have is that there could be "bias in selection, recording, or interpretation of events" (Happ et al. 2004, p. 243).

Data Mining and Analysis

Data mining predicts trends and behaviors. All of the questions lingering as to why your target group is not being reached can be answered speedily. For example, by interviewing those responsible for the youth outreach if you have one and directly observing through various means the scope of the program can help the leadership team predict trends and behaviors. Most often there are hidden patterns that are not seen and the process of data mining and analysis can take off the scale so to speak.

Data Mining and Collaboration

When developing a strategic plan, a strategic leader usually has the options of choosing to serve either as an expert, pair of hands, or to collaborate with all the stakeholders in addressing a problem (Block, 2002). My advice to local church pastors is to collaborate with all major stakeholders in developing the strategic plan for the local church. Collaborating with all stakeholders is appropriate because it emphasizes a joint effort in solving problems. The collaborative intervention allows everyone to be actively involved with the process either as collecting data, analysis, setting of goals, developing action plans, implementation as well as being responsible for every phase or aspect of the process. Decisions are jointly made based upon discussion and negotiations. The goal here is to make sure that problems that are solved remain solved and that the local church leadership team has the right skill to deal with any issue that might later arise.

To ensure the process of data mining and analysis is in no way undermined or obstructed, leadership must guide the process. Guiding the process does not mean undue control. It simply means that the local pastor along with the leadership team must highlight boundaries, benefits, and overall objectives of the strategic plan. The process is properly guided when leadership clearly communicate information required or data needed to determine the scope of the strategic plan, the roles of the each stakeholder, support the leadership team is willing to provide, and time schedule for the project.

Collaboration has the potential to strengthen the system. Too often, strategic plans fail to yield fruitful results because it is done either once a year or once every three to five years with no follow-ups or feedback to enhance or motivate performance once it is over with until the next planning. Nothing is usually done about the outcome of the previous plan or proposals, thereby neglecting the real purpose of the strategic plan. Most often there is no ongoing feedback or

STRATEGIC PLANNING

review of progress. Often the process is seen as a chore to be endured resulting into insufficient preparation time or effort.

Collaboration will help the local church establish current levels of performance and benchmark across departments or functions. Collaboration will help the strategic leader identify ways of improving performance, individually and collectively. Collaboration will also help the pastor set clear goals for the future while assessing potential and desire for development. Collaborating with all stake-holders can help the pastoral staff establish the appropriate means of motivation as well as improve communication throughout the local church.

Data collection and Analysis

Data-based problem identification is an important method because it can "be used to clarify a problem, to establish a baseline, and to measure the efficacy of interventions" (Burns 2004, p. 64). Data analysis enables the leadership team to detect patterns and implications as well as suggest application of the data (Block, 2002). To determine how to move forward, it would be better to start with any plan (not necessarily a strategic plan) either in the past or currently used if the local church has one.

To ensure proper analysis of the data collected, the leadership must be willing to spend some money on computer and software. Lots of software on data analysis are available and very useful. The qualitative data analysis software (QDAS) would be my recommendation. The QDAS software manages data by sorting them into manageable coding. Once the data are entered and codes assigned, the software shows similar codes at the same time as well as each piece of the data in relation to others. However, the lack of software should never be an excuse for not planning strategically. Most local churches do not have substantial data that are complicated. Thus, for the local church depending on the size, a good and effective strategic plan can be developed without the use of data analysis software. We did not use any software during the first and second strategic plans developed for Kingdom Harvest Ministries Inc. in Liberia in 2005 and 2007.

Whether data analysis software is used or not, data collected should help the local church in preparing a practical and reasonable strategic plan. To have a practical, realistic strategic plan, leadership must use data collected to establish levels of performance and benchmark across departments or functions. Data collected must be used to identify ways of improving performance, individually and collectively. Data should be analyzed so as to help the leadership set clear goals for the future as well as assess potential and desire for development and to establish the appropriate means of motivation. The best way to begin is to seek to improve communication throughout the organization.

Data collection will assure that the local church as a strategic organization plans for the future without assumptions. Why assume when you have all information necessary and related to the situation without obstruction? When you have adequate data, the organization can learn from the past to improve the future, build on successes and strengths, recognize individuals' strengths and abilities, identify areas to develop skills and knowledge, value individual contribution, and improve working relationships through clear communication.

Database

Every local church should have a database. The goal of having a database is to enable the effective organization of data collected so that its contents can easily be accessed, managed, and updated. The purpose of the database is to provide users the capabilities of controlling read and write access to the aggregations of data records or files and specifying report generation, as well as analyzing its use. Database is essential to the local church in that it shows pattern of how data collected was analyzed and integrated to align with the vision and mission of the local church.

Creating a database should not be troublesome and costly. Microsoft Access would be a better choice for the local church because it is easy to use and cost effective. The software can be installed without difficulty. It can be maintained with minimal effort, access from remote locations, and find support and documentation easily. It also reduces complexity and eliminates detail-oriented tasks.

Once a database has been established, every department can use it to both access and store information. According to McGill (2004), the purpose of database application is to offer "organizations better and more timely access to information, improved quality of information, improved decision making, reduced application development backlogs and improved information systems department/user relationships" (p. 41).

CHAPTER FOUR

THE IMPACT OF STRATEGIC PLANNING ON THE LOCAL CHURCH

The lack of strategic planning is a factor in the decline of conversion in the body of Christ. Even in churches with a strong outreach emphasis, discipleship is most often lacking because of the lack of strategic management. This chapter is intended to share light on the necessity of strategic planning within the local church. We will discuss how a church can grow through innovation using my mentor, Bishop Winker, and my pastoral experience as examples. The goal is to show that without strategic management in the local church, growth can turn to stagnation and multiple conversions cannot materialize into genuine discipleship.

The Role of Innovation in Strategic Management

Strategic leadership requires a willingness to explore new avenues and alternatives. The pastor as a strategic leader should have the capability to cope with change, be willing to always plan, and be in readiness to adapt to changing trends. There should always be a supportive working environment to encourage full participation of all stake-holders. When people feel a part of the process, innovation is possible and effective. The pastor should lead in creating the supportive environment that stimulates and enhances innovation.

For innovation to prevail within the local church, it is imperative that the pastoral staff creates a culture where new innovative ideas and methods are supported and encouraged. This type of culture is possible where the leader is willing and emotionally and intellectually prepared to challenge "the process, inspired vision, enabled others to act, [and] modeled the way" (Bass 1990, 218). Every leader needs to understand that creating a culture that is rich in support and direction is the breeding ground for innovation.

Innovation truly flourishes in a thriving organizational culture that is flexible, empowering, welcomes ideas, tolerates risk, celebrates success, fosters respect, and encourages fun. For such a culture to exist, these four things, leader-ship, people, basic values, and innovative values should be in effect.

Leadership

Leadership can shape attitudes and influence convictions and behaviors. As such, a leader can serve as a role model for many. As a role model, the leader can inspire trust and conviction in the followers. For example, when I was about thirteen years old, I met a leader that changed my outlook and enhanced my convictions. That leader is Bishop Isaac S. Winker of the Dominion Christian Fellowship in Monrovia, Liberia, West Africa. I first met Bishop Winker at a youth convention. The manner in which the bishop spoke and interacted with the young people was vastly different than the other speakers and even my pastor. Although Bishop Winker was in his late middle age at that time, he really understood the concerns of the young people and related to them more on their level than any person in the church. At a time when many young people were questioning the role of faith in their lives, Bishop Winker's style of leadership, which is more transformational in nature, influenced a lot of young people to rethink their priorities than any other of his peers in Liberia.

Another way Bishop Winker shaped attitudes and behaviors is by creating a culture of shared values that embraces creative thinking and breaking new grounds. The bishop's motivation was if his leadership team is happy, satisfied, dedicated, and energetic, they'll take good care of members within their department. When the members are happy, they will invite their friends and relatives to become a part of the church. Bishop Winker encouraged the young people to have fun, dress as they want, and have talent shows to help them spot out potentials and develop those potentials for the glory of God. As a result of this culture, Bishop Winker was able to change the mindset of the entire congregation, thereby affecting their outputs in a more proficient manner because of the culture of fun and celebration that prevailed without compromising biblical values and principles.

Bishop Winker was successful because his leadership revolves around relationships. At a time when most pas-tors were distrustful and suspicious of young people, he builds a relationship with them by embracing the creativity of the youthfulness. As the relationship deepens, people started to increase their confident and trust in the vision and strategies of the leader.

People

People are the strongest asset within any organization. Yet retaining strong and energetic members, especially the younger generation, seems to be a bigger problem today. Leaders need to be asking questions that will help them empower the strongest asset, people. Empowerment can be in the form of better incentive opportunities as a means of motivating younger workers to commit to the job or by "cultivat[ing] intensive one-on-one relationships and empathy for individuals" (Bass 1990, 218). As the leader develops this intensive relationship, the atmosphere would be created that can help the leader identify strong points in the membership and rotate them to different disciplines or assignments. Rotating staffs and members as a means of empowerment allows the staffs and members to experience different facets of the organization and then possibly make a choice of which discipline or department they would have the most impact (Bass 1990).

Empowering the younger generation seems to be a challenge for most organizations (Rezak 2004). Yet an innovative leader will explore every avenue to ensure that the younger generations are empowered, motivated, and firmly established in the culture of the organization. One classic example of such innovative leadership is Bishop Winker, who broke away from the traditions of the church to reach two groups of people, the younger generation and the intellectuals. He did not conform to the organizational hierarchy but courageously empowered others into the role of leadership. Whenever he saw a potential in someone, no matter the age barrier, something that is a big deal in Africa, he reaches out to the person and helps that person positions him/herself into realizing his/her dream. As a result, Bishop Winker had raised up senators, representatives, city majors, and business executives in his church that did serve Liberia well before, during, and after the civil war.

Since people are the strongest and most valuable asset within the local church, there should be an emphasis on a culture that rallies each person around the values of the organization. By rallying each person around the values of the local church, the strategic leader will encourage full participation on all levels of the church. The goal is to strengthen morale and motivate everyone to progressive action by enhancing a positive self-concept or image. For example, when developing the strategic plan for Kingdom Harvest Ministries Inc., Liberia, West Africa, in 2005, there was full participation on all levels of the organization. The process included a strategic planning workshop within each department, a series of interviews, as well as a critical and analytical review of the organization activities for the time under reviewed. Though this process encourages full participation, the goal is to set the framework from which every sector of the organization can be guided with respect to the strategic objectives. Having the right culture and creating an atmosphere of ownership where inputs are solicited and valued on all levels can breed innovation. The objective is to provide direction and enhance feedback and communication.

Basic Values

Values can impact how and why a person makes decisions. People will most likely choose practices and make decisions based upon their beliefs and values. Therefore, it is important that "whatever people intrinsically value, choosing the best practices that conduce to those values requires true belief " (Goldman 1999, 75).

Depending on the values of a leader, he/she could require every proposition to be justified by evidence before decisions can be made. Another leader could insist on creating an atmosphere of collaboration through consensus building depending on his values. Yet still another leader could focus on the processes used to strategize and move the organization forward (Goldman 1999). Benhabib (1992) is quoted by Goldman (1999) as saying that depending on the value of the leader, the process of decision making could require "each participant [to] have an equal chance to initiate and to continue communication; each must have an equal chance to make assertions, recommendations, and explanations; all must have equal chances to express their wishes, desires, and feelings" (p. 77).

Besides decision making, values can help shape the behavior of all stakeholders within an organization. Organizational values can ensure that all stakeholders relate to each other in a way that promotes a commitment to teamwork for higher productivity and efficiency and professionalism in all that is done in the name of the organization. Shared values can create an atmosphere of commitment to protect and safeguard the assets of the organization at all times. Organizational values can also influence behaviors in the areas of integrity, truthfulness, authenticity, and a commitment to treat one another with respect and dignity.

The shared values of an organization can either make or break the organization because "the backbone of the organization is the principles that define the organization, such as trust, respect, learning, commitment, inclusiveness and contribution" (Wycoff 2004, par. 6). A leader who can rally each worker around the values of the organization while being creative in implementing the strategic goals of the organization can lead the organization into having a competitive edge within society. The pastor as a strategic manager should know and communicate clearly the basic values of the local church. When the leadership team especially knows the basic values of the local church, they will take full ownership through a high degree of relational coordination and mutual respect. When the basic values of the local church is clearly communicated, it will strengthen the strategic goals, and everyone will make every effort to maintain their credibility and show that they care about what is happening at the church.

Innovation Values

Innovation should be the mindset of the culture of an organization that values creativity. A culture that pro-motes innovation is one in which people can freely express new ideas and perceptions. For innovation to prevail, it is important that the leader creates a culture where new innovative ideas and methods are supported and encouraged. This type of culture is possible where the leader is willing and emotionally and intellectually prepared to challenge "the process, inspired vision, enabled others to act, [and] modeled the way" (Bass 1990, 218). Every leader needs to understand that creating a culture that is rich in support and direction is the breeding ground for innovation. This type of culture heightens trust, respect, and high standards. It also stimulates intellectualism and encourages a stronger coaching and mentoring relationship.

Innovative leadership encourages full participation and enhances performance through a healthy interpersonal relationship that strengthens morale and motivates others to progressive action. As a young pastor in the 1990s, at a time when many young people in Liberia, West Africa, were questioning the role of faith in their lives due to the civil war, I rallied them around biblical values and principles by encouraging full participation in the decision making process within the church. I wanted new and fresh ideas to reach the young people who were daily being lured to join one of the warring factions. I sorted out those who were still committed to the church and have not yet join the fighting forces to give me ideas as to what approach to take in encouraging young people from joining the rebel groups and killing innocent people. By doing so, I was able to enhance commitment and performance through a healthy interpersonal relationship that strengthens morale and motivated others by encouraging them to pursue their dreams without compromising their faith.

The focus and emphasis of strategic leadership is not control or power but getting others motivated to positively contribute to the process. Bass (2003) states that leadership "requires motivating and inspiring, keeping people moving in the right direction, despite major obstacles to change, by appealing to basic but often untapped human needs, values, and emotions" (p. 46). In the early days of my pastoral leadership, despite major objections from other pastors and leaders, I motivated young people to put education second to godliness. I told the young people that the best way to impact their communities and be the light of the world was to pursue college education. I counseled young people to give the issue of marriage a careful thought before committing. Most importantly, the young people were motivated to participate in the decision making process and the direction of the church. This example is given here to show that one of the outcomes of transformational leadership is empowerment through "relationship between individuals…oriented to social vision and change, not [just the stipulated] organizational goals" (Lawlor 2006, par. 11).

As stated at the beginning of this chapter, without strategic management in the local church, growth can turn to stagnation and multiple conversions cannot materialize into genuine discipleship. I will prove this point by using my own ministerial experience as a case study.

My Years as Senior Pastor of the Monrovia Open Bible Church in Liberia (1992–1999)

When I took over the leadership of the church, the membership was at 150. As stated earlier, at a time when many young people in Liberia, West Africa, were questioning the role of faith in their lives due to the civil war, I rallied them around biblical values and principles by encouraging full participation in the decision making process within the church. I also drastically moved away from what we term in Liberia as missionary mentality (limited education and early marriage because you are a Christian) despite major objections from other leaders within the church's circle. I even allowed girls to come to church in trousers or whatsoever they could afford since those city girls did not have church dresses. I did not pressure the young people in the church to marry early as most pas-tors did. Instead, I counseled those who were dating and encouraged them to give the issue of marriage a careful thought before committing. I motivated young people to put education second to godliness. I encouraged young people to pursue college education as a strategic means of being empowered to serve their communities and country well. I treated both old and young alike with respect and held them to a higher standard and accountability. And I delegated responsibilities and supported my team of leaders with needed resources and emotionally.

From November 1992 to April 1999 when I resigned from the leadership of that local church, we had three services each Sunday. We planted eight new churches and established a high school and Bible college. We had a radio ministry and a powerful young ministry. I held three seminars each year, three mission conferences each year, and multiple church-planting crusades each year. We have a great ministry with the Armed Forces of Liberia including a Bible Training Center that led many in the military to the Lord. Some are even serving as full-time pastors today.

Yet with all this so-called growth, because we did not have a strategic plan, we could not sustain the growth and my desire for intentional discipleship was never realized. Fulltime-paid staff grew from three persons to thirty-eight. Funds were always available to support everything we did without any outside support in the midst of war. Yet because we lack a basic strategic plan, we could not transform the multiple decisions into genuine, intentional disciples for Christ as we desired.

Church leaders, we need to understand that strategic leadership enables people to cope effectively with the effects and impacts of change within an organization. Strategic management enables an organization to align the "what and why" of the organization with the "how and when" thereby enabling those within the organization to better cope with changing trends so as to strategize for maximum impact. Because there was a lack of strategic management, we were unable to align the "what and why" of the local church with the "how and when." As a result, the organization was not better equipped to cope with the rapid growth and changes we were experiencing.

When strategic leadership is lacking, it becomes difficult to establish and affirm a sense of identity for the organization. Without a strategic plan, we cannot offer an appealing future vision. Although there might be progress, without a strategic plan, the local church cannot develop a deep collective identity that heightens both individual and collective self-efficacy (Conger 1999). Due to an internal conflict between the denominational hierarchy, I resigned from the pastorate of the church in which I was experiencing rapid growth in April of 1999. To avoid a major split, I submitted my resignation one year in advance and worked with the denominational and local leadership to ensure a smooth transition. Yet because there was no strategic plan in place, the transition did not go as smoothly as we had hoped. People were apprehensive about the future of the church. Although the denomination has a year to prepare for my exit, the lack of a strategic plan made it difficult to offer an appealing vision for the future without my leadership. Although we had a well-attended farewell service, tensions were high and feelings were hurt on both sides. I preached a sermon entitled separation is necessary using the story of Paul and Barnabas. I was given gifts and praised for my leadership by the denominational leader-ship. Yet right after the service, people were insulting one another and making the most derogatory statements to one another. If we have had a strategic plan as to how to move the congregation along smoothly, the episode of that day would have been avoided.

Initial Phase of KHM (1999–2004)

After I resigned from the open Bible denomination, I established the Kingdom Harvest Ministries Inc. as a church-planting movement. Within a year, we had three churches and a junior high school. Plans were being made to establish another church in one of the cities and to start a high school at the headquarters church. My trusted leadership coupled with my zeal and teachings on church planting and intentional discipleship led to rapid growth more than it was when I was at my former church. Within the initial stage of operation, I left Liberia for the USA on a conference. While in the USA, another phase of the war broke out in Liberia. As a result,

I could not return and, within a year, got a diversity visa (a permanent resident visa) for my family to move to the USA.

Because I left Liberia without a strategic plan, the new leadership was unable to align the "what" and "why" of the organization with the "how" and "when." As a result of the lack of strategic leadership, the leadership team and members of Kingdom Harvest Ministries were not enabled to better cope with changing trends so as to strategize for maximum impact. The leadership now was more focus on control and power instead of getting the members motivated to positively contribute to the process. The lack of a strategic plan that would have served as a road map created a situation in which every leader was doing what he felt was best without coordination and cooperation. As a result, the ministry could not keep moving in the right direction. There was a decline in membership, the junior high school was closed down and all resources and efforts focused on the high school at the headquarters church. Between 2000 to 2004, two of the pastors broke away with their congregations. There were constant tensions between the pastoral staffs at the headquarters church. Instead of becoming a church-planting movement, KHM was struggling for survival. Although I visited Liberia once every year during this crisis period and helped to put some things in place for the two weeks I am there, change was never effective. We lost a lot of money on programs that did not work. It seems as though we had major obstacles to change, and the leadership was unable to appeal to the basic but often untapped human needs, values, and emotions of the people.

Some of you reading this might say that the example given is a result of leadership gap due to my abrupt departure from the scene as the visionary. But as we shall discuss later, the problem was more than a void in leader-ship. It was the impact of the lack of strategic leadership. It is said that people "behave in ways that seek to establish and affirm a sense of identity for [themselves]" (Conger 1999, 145). If we had a strategic plan, the leadership team in my absence would have been forced to coordinate their efforts and cooperate with one another. The strategic plan would not only be a road map, it would have established a sense of identity for the group. The strategic plan would have force the leadership to become strategic in all that they do. As strategic leaders, they would have tied their sense of identity to the goals and collective experiences associated with the missions of KHM, thereby changing perceptions of the nature of the work itself, offering an appealing future vision, developing a deep collective identity, and heightening both individual and collective self- efficacy.

Benefits of Strategic Management within the Local Church

The primary benefit the local church will reap by embracing strategic management is that the church will become a change agent. Every local church is to become a change agent within the community. If the local church will be relevant in a postmodern world, there must be a shift toward strategic management. Jesus said His church is to be wise as a serpent and harmless as a dove. It is wisdom that will make the church more relevant than anything the world offers today. For the local church to become a true change agent within the community, leadership must put in place a plan that will help them make concise and clear decisions in a timely manner, especially in critical and stressful times. This process requires cultivating self-discipline and continuously scrutinizing and improving the decision-making process with the goal of eliminating confusion and dramatically increasing clarity (Kopeikina 2006).

To become a change agent within the community, the church must set the pace of tying innovation and transformational leadership together. In other words, the church must emphasize a culture that rallies each member around the values of the organization while being creative in implementing the business strategy (missions) of the organization. The process of rallying each member around the values of the organization is possible when the leader views himself/herself as being in partnership with each member of the organization. This partnership is expanded through a mentoring and coaching relationship with the goal of bringing out the best in each person.

The church must develop a plan that will encourage involvement in grassroots community initiatives with-out alienating the unchurched. If we are to be harmless as dove as Jesus said, we must use wisdom in attracting people to the Lord. Jesus was not judgmental in dealing with people. He affected the lives of everyone everywhere He went and brought about meaningful change. The religious establishment of His days was always angry because of how Jesus reached out to those who needed salvation. Why can't we do the same?

For the Kingdom Harvest Ministries in Liberia, one of the ways we are proactively working to be a change agent within every community where we have an entity is through a periodic review of the strategic plan that was first developed in 2005. Realizing that critical to the successful attainment of an organization's vision is an effective and well-implemented strategy, the strategic plan will be periodically reviewed on all levels of the organization to ensure that the long-term objectives are properly aligned with the mission and core values of the organization. This is because I acknowledge the fact that a strategy that is well-developed and properly implemented can position an organization to launch successfully into its future. In achieving the foregoing, we will review the strategic plan quarterly on all levels. The process will include a strategic planning workshop within each department, a series of interviews, as well as a critical and analytical review of the organization activities for the time under reviewed. Though this process encourages full participation, the goal is to set the framework from which every sector of the organization can be guided with respect to the strategic objectives. This plan sets a stage for new insights, ideas, and unexpected breakthrough because the culture creates an atmosphere in which people will be "physically relaxed, emotionally positive, happy, released from fear and anxiety; charged with power, success, self-confidence, and energy, totally in the present, and mentally focused on the task at hand" (Kopeikina 2006, 2).

Another benefit of strategic management in the local church is that the leadership will create a culture of ownership. Having the right culture and creating an atmosphere of ownership where inputs are solicited and valued on all levels can breed innovation. Leadership must have a strategy that can enhance the culture of innovation. The strategy is to solicit inputs from internal and external stakeholders because the concept "that create a break-through requires a process of looking outside and inside; at customers, suppliers, and competitors; at changes in demographics, trends, economics, regulations, and political environments" (Wycoff 2004, par. 7). The goal of soliciting external input is to build upon the concepts and put a strategy in place by the leadership to ensure that the concepts as amended be effectively implemented. The strategy of implementation will discuss how resources will be attained and allocated for smooth operation. Benchmarks will be set along with short- and long-term goals that are measurable and can lead to proficiency. The objective is to provide direction and enhance feedback and communication in the innovative process.

Making decisions with clarity in a fast and easier manner is another benefit we reap by embracing strategic management within the local church. This process requires that records be kept of all difficult decisions. The objective is to stimulate insightfulness and innovation in every decision making process. The records will help the organization determine why the issue was difficult and how effective was the methods employed. This process will help the leadership team "see patterns and will gain critical information about how [we] learned to make decisions…and what decision-making habits [were] developed over time" (Kopeikina 2006, 1).

Embracing strategic management will enable the local church to develop an implementation strategy of any strategic plan. A strategic plan is only as good as its implementation strategy. A well-developed and properly implemented strategy is the key to launching any organization successfully into its future. As such, strategic leadership focuses on strategies that can enhance efficient imple-mentation. The implementation strategy will serve as a strategic road map to help align the leadership plan with realities and trends. The implementation strategy will help the leadership of the local church do the following:

1. Set milestones that will enable the realization of the vision.
2. Define strategic alternatives and corresponding goals that will enhance the realization of the vision.
3. Ensure control and evaluation of the entire process.

4. Ensure accountability as responsibilities are clearly defined and those responsible for implementation clearly identified.
5. Create an opportunity for milestones to be monitored and evaluated.

Strategic management encourages diversity. Diversity has the potential of breeding innovation. Therefore, the leadership should encourage every style of thinking, perspectives, and experiences to ensure that the atmosphere is conducive for innovation. However, leadership must realize and make it clear that it is not possible to implement every idea from all stakeholders. Therefore the strategy of implementation will include guidelines for evaluating ideas and preventing going over the edge on a seductive idea that doesn't fit.

Strategic management enhances global outreach. An old adage states that no man is an island. Survival and success depend to a greater extend on interaction and interrelationship with others. Many organizations today are interacting and interrelating with others in a global society through projects, cultural, political, geographical, and other elements for survival and success. The church must learn to interact and interrelate with others within the body of Christ for a global outreach.

Domestic and Global Outreaches

A global outreach is different in characteristics to that of a domestic outreach or project basically due to the fact that it is a crisscross of functions, work locale, market, culture, and products. Strategic management and planning will create the avenue for the local church to approach the outreach efforts with flexibility, effective communication, projection of values, and promoting teamwork over individual performance. With global outreach or project comes language, cultural, custom, geographical, political, communication, and even ethical barriers.

Both domestic and global outreaches must be well planned and do need a specific goal and time frame to be effective and successful. Domestic and global outreaches need to be well managed, evaluated, and audited to ensure a successful and satisfactory completion. Be it domestic or global, no project should become a perpetual pro-gram; instead, they ought to have a definite ending that is properly described during the planning stage. Domestic and global projects can be hampered by issues like poor planning. Not clearly defining a project and making poor decisions and inadequate communication during the planning stage can serve as a barrier that could hamper a project. Another hindrance could be poor scheduling. If schedules are not adhered to and meetings are not often held, a project can be greatly hampered. Poor organization is a platform for failure. If the project is not properly organized and managed, if responsibilities are not properly delegated and people are not held accountable, the structure of the project can suffer a lot making it impossible to keep up with the timeline and resource management. Lack of direction can slow the progress of the project or outreach efforts. If the task required to close the project are not well coordinated, if responsibilities are not fully communication, if the leadership cannot tell or direct how to begin and end the project or outreach efforts, and if there is no commitment as to how the project would be delivered, its success is bound to be hampered. For projects to be successful there must be control. Monitoring and follow-ups are keys to controlling the project or recognizing problems associated with the project (Gray 2002).

There are challenges associated with global outreach. Many churches in the West have either a direct outreach program or are in mission partnerships with churches in Africa and/or developing countries. We will discuss some of the challenges so as to drive home the essential need of strategic management within the local church. Some of the challenges are controlling progress, communication, bonding as a group, and getting assigned tasks done in a timely manner. The examples given are based on real experiences with Kingdom Harvest Ministries in Liberia and a local church here in the USA. The examples are given to help churches and organizations that are in partnership with churches or organizations in other parts of the world to minimize loss and improve efficiency. I hope and pray that no one reading this would misunderstand the point intended. If that happens, then I have not communicated well. Having said that, let us consider some of the challenges associated with global outreach.

The most important challenge is that of communication. The success of any project lies with proper communication. When undertaking a global outreach or project, we need to keep in mind that clarity is of essence. If communication is not clear, misunderstanding could gravely impede the progress of the project or outreach. For example, a local church here in the USA has been in partner-ship with Kingdom Harvest Ministries in Liberia, West Africa. In 2008, a 40 ft container was sent to Liberia with assorted items for the churches, building materials for a church our partner was helping us to erect, as well as tools to be used both for the construction and a vocational school. When the manifest for the container was sent to the leadership in Liberia, a note was attached that read, "Do not take to the port, for distribution purpose only." As a result of that note, the process of getting the container from the Port of Monrovia was delayed. When the port authority requested for the manifest of items in the container, the leadership in Liberia had nothing to work with although they had the completed manifest with them. That note created difficulty for the team in Liberia. As a result of the lack of clarity, the container was held at the port until we arrived in Liberia in 2009. It took me four days to finally get the container out of the port and the payment of a fine for not fully disclosing all items on the container. Some of the items like a 200 KVA generator and some bikes were removed from the container until the fine was paid before it was released to us. If only that note was not included when the manifest was sent, we would never have experienced all of the difficulties we encountered. What that note should have said was "Use this same information for distribution." When the manifest was compiled, it was done in a manner that would be distribution of the items to the various churches and schools easier.

Another challenge with global outreach or project would be controlling the progress of the project. This can be taken care of by establishing ground rules at the beginning of the project and developing a tracking system that would ensure that everyone is on the same pace. The tracking system can be used by the project manager to encourage more participation and give focus and direction to the project. For example, in 2009, a team from the USA travelled with me to Liberia for the construction of a church building. Prior to that trip, while in Liberia in 2007, the pastor (a man who loves the people of Liberia and motivated his local church to partner with KHM), who was a guest of our 2007 convention in Liberia, promised that his local church would help us build a one-thousand-seat sanctuary we had been praying to have constructed in a area that was ripe for a new church. When he returned to the USA, he motivated and mobilized his congregation. Fund was raised and sent to Liberia for the purchase of the land and the laying of the foundation for the building.

To control and track the progress of the project, the leadership team in Liberia decided that after the foundation, the next phase would be the planting of pillars and then the roof. However, the team in Liberia did not put in place a ground rule at the beginning of the project. As a result of the lack of establishing a ground rule, coupled with excitement that a new church was being built in partnership from the USA, coordination was very loosed. The pastor of the church being constructed and his leadership team did not coordinate with the project team (a group of interdisciplinary professionals that handles all projects in Liberia) of KHM. Due to this lack of coordination, tension developed between the project team and the leadership of the local church. The tension caused the project team to back off, leaving people who did not know much about project management in charge. As a result, resources were not properly allocated, and the original plan of how to proceed was neglected, causing setbacks. The construction was never completed in the time frame initially set by the project team. I am sure pastors reading this book and others who have had partnership in developing countries can attest to the facts that projects are most often never completed on time. We can address this concern by establishing ground rules at the beginning of the project and developing a tracking system that would ensure that everyone is on the same pace.

Cultural sensitivity is also a challenge with global out-reach. Working with people from multiple ethnic and sociopolitical backgrounds is never easy. The structure and nature of the team posed some serious challenges. It is essential for the success of the team and the implementation of the project that the project manager be fully aware of the cultural differences and possesses the proper etiquette in projecting

STRATEGIC PLANNING

a global project. This awareness will help avoid social issues that could negatively affect the outcome or progress of the project (Ray 2004).

I will continue with the example of Kingdom Harvest Ministries in Liberia to show how the lack of cultural sensitivity can negatively affect the outcome of a global outreach. In 2009, a team went to Liberia with me as we had hoped to complete the building of a one-thousand-seat sanctuary. The plan (although not fully followed as stated above) was to erect the pillars after the foundation of the building. Once the pillars are in, the roof would be put in. The goal was to ensure that funds from the USA were wisely used. Since most of the members in the new church were young and students, if money from oversea is spent on major aspects of the building, it would be easier to complete the project on time. When the team from the USA arrived in Liberia, their goal as it appears was to lay bricks (take up the walls of the building). When the leader of the team from the USA did not find any brick on site, he was furious.

He shared his disappointment with members of the leadership in Liberia before even talking to me. Culturally, when an authority is upset, people will do everything to appease the authority by going with his wishes. While I was at the Port of Monrovia trying to get the container I mentioned earlier out, the pastor of the local church got some of his members together and they decided to get bricks. Within an hour, they got about US$3,000 worth of bricks on the site. The team from the USA was happy, and everybody started to lay bricks. There was great excitement, but one problem was about to linger and delay the completion of the project.

The plan for the building was designed here in the United States. The main sanctuary had no supporting pillars. That means steel trusses for the roof. With fund that the team took with them to Liberia now being spent on brick, cement, and everything needed to take up the walls, the roof was neglected. Now we have a building to roof level, but locally, it is difficult to raise US$10,000 for steel trusses. If the head of the team from the USA had understood that in our culture, when a leader is upset, people normally would not take the time to explain why but would just get on board, we would have completed the building on time. It is easier to take up the walls of a building once the pillars and the roof are in place. Even if US$100 now and then is raised, you can buy bricks with that amount. With the roof, it takes skill, and the company hired to build the roof is not willing to take a $100 here and there. They want about 60 percent down and the rest down when they are done. If only someone has called me while at the port, we could have avoided that mistake. The purpose of this example is not to cast blame but to point out that cultural sensitivity is a huge challenge with global outreach. Working with people from multiple ethnic and sociopolitical backgrounds is never easy. It is essential for the successful implementation of the project that people be fully aware of the cultural differences. This awareness will help avoid social issues that could negatively affect the outcome or progress of the project.

A global project can be effective if project managers learn to build relationships through the correct protocol and process. They must seek out practical insights about the culture in which the project is been conducted as a proactive step in helping the organization to be more suc-cessful with the overseas operations. Seeking out knowl-edge about the culture can lead the project manager and other team members from assumption. However, the knowledge gained should not be used by project man-agers and organizations to develop a

STRATEGIC PLANNING

stereotype that can lead to embarrassing behaviors and slow down progress. More importantly, project managers need to ensure that all team members respect one another and relate to each other appropriately.

CHAPTER FIVE

UNDERSTANDING ORGANIZATIONAL PARADIGMS AND ADAPTING TO MAXIMIZE RELEVANCY IN A POSTMODERN WORLD

Organizational paradigms is about the approaches organizations employ to facilitate the decision-making process in a manner that enhances efficiency and productivity. Although every organization is unique, the structures and organizational designs are propelled by the paradigm. There are basically three strategic organizational para-digms, namely rational, natural, and open systems (an overview of each is given within this chapter). While pur-suing my doctoral degree in organizational leadership, one of my tasks was to create a new organizational paradigm and analyze the ways in which an existing organization could operate within that paradigm. That new paradigm is the subject of another book and my doctoral dissertation. What I hope to do in this chapter is to show how strategic management can enhance the organizational paradigm of the local church in a way that can help the church sustain itself and adapt for the future to include shifts in structures and processes.

An Overview of Current Organizational Paradigms

There are three classifications of organizational paradigms. They are rational, natural, and open systems. In comparing and contrasting the organizational paradigms, Scott and Davis (2007) stressed that both the rational and natural systems approach view organizations as a "closed system, separate from its environment and encompassing a set of stable and easily identified participants" (p. 31) but that "the three perspectives partially conflict, partially overlap, and partially complement one another" (p. 32). The open system emphasizes the interrelationship and connection between the organization and its environment whereas "organizational goals and their relation to the behavior of participants are much more problematic for the natural than the rational system theorist" (p. 60).

The Rational System

The rational system focuses on both the distinctive characteristics and normative structures of the organization. Scott and Davis (2007) classify the rational system as being "highly formalized collectivities oriented to the pursuit of specific goals" (p. 34). The rational system is formalized with the goal of "mak[ing] behavior more predictable by standardizing and regulating it" (p. 37). The essence of regulating behavior is to "permits stable expectations" (p. 37). The formalized structure as practiced by the rational system enables employees to diagram the social structures and the work flows, allowing them to depict these relationships and processes with the possibility of consciously manipulating them—designing and redesigning the division of responsibilities, the flow of information or materials, or the ways in which participants report to one another (p. 38).

The emphasis of the rational system is not formulating goals but designing the proper strategy to enhance the implementation of goals. Mannheim (1950) is cited in Scott and Davis (2007) as clarifying that the rational system focuses on "the extent to which a series of actions is organized in such a way as to lead to predetermined goals with maximum efficiency" (p. 35).

The Natural System

The natural system focuses on common attributes and interests of the organization. According to Scott and Davis (2007), the emphasis is on creating an atmosphere for collaboration and cooperative partnership to enhance "organizational stability and continuity" (p. 30). Thus the natural system can be classified "as [a] social systems, forged by consensus or conflict, seeking to survive" (p. 34). The desire or need to survive often pushes organizations that adhere to the natural system approach to not devote their "full resources to producing products or services; [but rather] each must expend energies maintaining itself " (p. 60). The need for continuity causes the leadership to concentrate their efforts of "what is done rather than what is decided or planned" (p. 62).

The Open System

The open system emphasizes the interrelationship and connection between the organization and its environment (Scott and Davis, 2007). The open system paradigm can be summed up "as activities involving coalitions of participants with varying interests embedded in wider environments" (p. 34). Swinth (1974) is cited in Scott and Davies (2007) as implying that an open system organization could be viewed as cybernetic when there is an emphasis on the "importance of the operations, control, and policy centers, and the flows among them" (p. 91). Buckley (1967) is cited by Scott and Davies (2007) as stating that the cybernetic system is "goal-directed [and not] goal oriented" (p. 92).

Each organizational paradigm stresses the need for structure and behavior slightly differently but each "partially overlap, and partially complement one another" (Scott and Davis 2007, 32). Either the emphasis is on being goal oriented, goal directed, or behavior driven. What is important is that each seeks to promote a pattern that will enhance better decision and proficiency on all levels of the organization.

Strategic Management and Organizational Paradigm

Strategic management when properly understood and implemented can help the local church in many ways. Strategic management ties innovation and transformational leadership together. When there is a strong support network within the denominational hierarchy, the local pastor can be innovative without fear of falling out of grace with the leadership of the denomination. Denominational leaders need to realize that every pastor needs a pastor who can serve as a mentor and coach with the goal of bringing out the best in the pastor. Thus churches need to emphasize a paradigm that encourages flexible partner-ship and collaboration. By encouraging flexible partner-ship and collaboration, local pastors are encouraged to be opened to new ideas from each member of the team.

Strategic management with its emphasis on partner-ship, collaboration, and creativity will produce the right culture and create an atmosphere of ownership where inputs are solicited and valued on all levels of the organization or local church. Strategic management focuses on both internal and external partnerships. The system requires that every idea or concept be written and submit-ted for discussion within the team. Since "innovation that begins with an internal brainstorming session will seldom result in anything other than pale, incremental concepts" (Wycoff 2004, par. 7), strategic management pro-motes soliciting inputs from external stakeholders as well because the concept "that create a breakthrough requires a process of looking outside and inside; at customers, suppliers, and competitors; at changes in demographics, trends, economics, regulations, and political environments (Wycoff 2004, par. 7). The goal of soliciting external input is to build upon the concepts and put a strategy in place by the team to ensure that the concepts as amended be effectively implemented. The strategy of implementation will discuss how resources will be attained and allocated for smooth operation. Benchmarks will be set along with short- and long-term goals that are measurable and can lead to proficiency.

Diversity of thoughts and concepts has the potential of breeding innovation. Thus, strategic management encourages every style of thinking, perspectives, and experiences to ensure that the atmosphere is conducive for innovation. It is important to note that every idea from all stakeholders cannot be implemented at once. Therefore the strategy of implementation will include guidelines for evaluating ideas and preventing going over the edge on a seductive idea that doesn't fit.

The focus and emphasis of strategic management is not control or power but getting others motivated to positively contribute to the process. Motivating others to action and ownership through full participation could bring forth transformation in any organization and is a breeding ground for innovation. To enable a higher level of performance, strategic management proposes that friendly partnership and collaboration can be effective when leadership adapt the following approach in the decision-making process.

1. Confirm the objective by asking and focusing on what is the purpose. How does it align with the team's goal?
2. Establish team awareness with understanding. This step will identify and record perceived problems/issues that may need to be addressed.
3. Conduct individual/team behavioral profiling; this step is one which involves the assessment of all the team members personalities in terms of their "transactional styles, leadership styles, learning/thinking styles, conflict resolution styles and stressors/value systems" (Ekman and Giangregorio 2003, 2). Creating a team profile will strengthen the team's culture.
4. Prepare experiential learning event schedule based on the facilitator's knowledge of the objectives.
5. Experiential learning—the facilitator can execute the experiential learning event schedule by "using the cornerstones of building trust, respect, open communication and interdependency" (Ekman and Giangregorio 2003, 2). He or she can wrap it all up by "recording what was learned, list expected benefits

and create an action plan which addresses the issues identified" (Ekman and Giangregorio 2003, 2).
6. Establish peak performance; this will reflect "a baseline benchmark of individual/team performance prior to the coalescence program, positioning after the coalescence program, indicate performance improvement strategies and measure performance" (Ekman and Giangregorio 2003, 2).
7. Benefits realization—after a specified amount of time, the team will meet to determine where they are on the performance map. The focus will be on "celebrat[ing] success and understanding, revisiting and addressing failure" (Ekman and Giangregorio 2003, 2).

As stated earlier, strategic management ties innovation and transformational leadership together. Innovation is effective and possible within a supportive working environment. Transformational leadership provides the supportive environment that stimulates and enhances innovation. Transformational leadership enhances performance through a healthy interpersonal relationship by encouraging full participation, which strengthens morale and motivates others to progressive action. Innovation is about change. Coping with change is never an easy task and requires planning and possible adaptation to changing trends on the part of leadership.

In order to achieve greater knowledge and capabilities and remain a viable entity, local churches will need to be proactive in creating a culture where new innovative ideas and methods are supported and encouraged. Bass (1990) notes that innovation is possible when organizations challenge "the process, inspired vision, enabled others to act, modeled the way and encouraged the heart" (p. 218). Strategic management when adapted and implemented will enhance the capacity of the local churches in creating a culture that is rich in support and direction.

Organizations that have thriving cultures are breeding grounds for innovation. Wycoff (2004) characterizes thriving organizational culture as an environment that "is flexible, empowering, welcomes ideas, tolerates risk, celebrates success, fosters respect and encourages fun" (para. 4). Strategic management will enable the local church and any organization to develop a thriving culture thereby creating an atmosphere of creativity and innovation.

Strategic management will help the local church be more focused and logical in its approach and the decision making process. Strategic management is intended to fill in gaps to the existing structure, validate existing knowledge by new researchers, expand knowledge with new ideas, broaden the perspectives of those who voices are minimized, and add to the body of knowledge (Creswell 2005) on providing quality of care by presenting new ideas that are practical and can improve the process of creativity within a highly regulated organization as the church. Strategic management will enhance the ability of senior pastors to "practice habits of thought that reflect sound reasoning—finding correct premises, testing the connections between their facts and assumptions, making claims based on adequate evidence" (Cooper and Schindler 2002, 32).

Innovation, creativity, partnership, and collaboration revolve around relationships. The strength and success of a relationship, especially in the local church depend on the level of confidence and trust members of the team have in the vision and strategies of the leader. However, it takes more than the leader just articulating clearly the vision and strategies of the organization. It also involves the tonality, enthusiasms, and convictions of the leader that he or she is able to transmit to the team. The leader, thus, acts as a role model in how he or she transmits the appropriate attitudes, behaviors, and convictions.

Currently, most local churches are expected by their denominations to make sure members are knowledgeable of the mission, goals, shared values, and ethical standards of the church or denomination. In some churches, for example the Kingdom Harvest Ministries churches in Liberia, West Africa, the leadership team interacts with one another and discuss the mission, goals, shared values, and ethical standards. This level of communication has increased efficiency as leaders are aware of boundaries, expectation, and the specific goals related to KHM becoming a continuous church planting movement. Such interaction between leaders ensure that "the smooth functioning of the organization is to some degree made independent of the feelings—negative or positive—that particular members have for one another" (Scott and Davis 2007, 38).

Scott and Davis (2007) state that alienation, inequity, insecurity, and overconformity often pose the greatest problem or potential problem for any organization. Two of the four problems (alienation and overconformity) cited by Scott and Davis (2007) pose potential problems for many local churches. Some local pastors are so concern about compliance to denominational regulations that their approach has alienated the community in which they minister. Other pastors are preoccupied with competition that their programs have become a combination of the best approaches from every service center without seeking input or collaboration from anyone.

Strategic management will redesign the structure and designs of the local church by empowering senior pastors to "practice habits of thought that reflect sound reasoning—finding correct premises, testing the connections between their facts and assumptions, making claims based on adequate evidence" (Cooper and Schindler 2002, 32). This redesign requires seeking partnership and collaboration on all levels of the organization. As such members on all levels will feel they are a valuable member of the team as their inputs will be given careful attention and analysis. More importantly, senior pastors will not have to alienate the leadership team from any form of decision making.

Pastors who are driven with internal competition by making the leadership team to overly conform to so-called best practices often subconsciously undermine cooperation and collaboration. Since strategic management encourages every style of thinking, perspectives, and experiences to ensure that the atmosphere is conducive for innovation, pastors would be forced to constantly solicit input on all levels of the local church and denomination.

An organization's greatest asset is its people. Leaders should be able to empower the members of the organization by relating to each member. A key to organizational success is individualized consideration, which includes how the leader develops, advises, and coaches the team members on an individual basis. There is a need within the local church for leaders to deal empathically with each individual's needs, abilities, and aspirations. This requires good listening and communication skills. Bass (1990) states that leaders need to "cultivate intensive one-on-one relationships and empathy for individuals" (p. 218). The stronger the perception of individuality is felt among the members, the higher the spirit and the commitment will be for the organization.

The local church today is overwhelmed with unresponsiveness from the community in which it ministers.

Strategic management has the potential to minimize unresponsiveness because the focus is on both internal and external partnerships. According to Wycoff (2004), the backbones of the organization are the principles that define the organization, "such as trust, respect, learning, commitment, inclusiveness and contribution" (para. 6). The values and principles of the organization cannot just be stated; they must be acted out in their behavior and interactions with the team members and community. The reputation of the local church will directly affect the response of the community. People feel good about aligning or becoming a part of a church that stands behind what they say and do both within and outside of the walls.

CHAPTER SIX

STRATEGY FORMULATIONS AND IMPLEMENTATIONS

Critical to the successful attainment of an organization's vision is an effective and well-implemented strategy. A strategy that is well developed and properly implemented can position an organization to launch successfully into its future. For a strategy to become effective, it should meet two requirements:

1. It should be aligned with the vision of the organization, that is, the long-term objectives should be aligned with the mission and core values of the organization. This can be done by conducting research on both the external and internal environments so as to make sure the long-term objectives are suited to the internal situations and external environment of the organization. This is important because long-term objectives serve as a basic to the strategy formulation of the organization.
2. It should have a well-developed implementation strategy that has SMART objectives. Once long-term

objectives are identified, the implementation strategy should be SMART to be effective. This can be done by asking the following questions:

- Are the objectives of this implementation strategy *simple* enough for everyone to grasp?
- Are they *motivational* enough to move everyone to action?
- Are they *agreeable and attainable* within the time frame?
- Are they *realistic* enough to achieve the desired results?
- And do they have proper time frame, or do they have the proper time limits to ensure adequate implementation?

In developing a strategic plan, careful analysis should be done within the internal and external environments of the local church to ensure that the strategic initiatives are relevant to trends within the community as well as situations within the culture and system of the local church. This can be done by conducting both a strength, weakness, opportunities, and threats (SWOT) analysis and matched pair analysis because the goal is to have more strategic options or alternatives for effectively implementing the strategies developed. The SWOT analysis identifies the internal strengths and weaknesses of the organization as well as the external opportunities and threats facing the organization. A matched pair analysis extends the scope of the SWOT analysis and provides more alternative for the strategic plan development.

Based upon the external and internal analysis, long-term objectives can be identified. The long-term objectives are expected to define the growth parameter of the local church for a period of one to three years. If the implementation plan is adhered to, the strategic plan will align the mission strategies with the vision and long-term objectives, enable the local church set milestones that will enhance the realization of the vision, define strategic alternatives and corresponding goals that will enhance the realization of the vision, and as well as define the strategic initiatives the local church has to undertake in other to consolidate its position within the community.

Environmental Analysis

To strategically position an organization, cope with changing trends, and have a competitive edge, it is imperative to not only understand the internal factors but also the external factors that have the potential to either make or break the organization. The external factors that influence, impact, and affect organizations "form the basis of the opportunities and threats that a firm faces in its competitive environment" (Pearce-Robinson 2003, 57).

The environmental analysis will help the local church identifies the strengths, weaknesses, opportunities, and threats. While the internal environment addresses how the local church has adapted or is adapting to trends within its denominational compact, the external environment will address present trends within the community or part of the world in which the local church exists and ministers. An analysis of the internal environment will help to identify the strengths and weaknesses and the external environment analysis will help identify opportunities and threats that the local church will have to address within the next one to three years. Based upon environmental analysis, long-term objectives can be identified that can propel the local church into its future without compromising its message and values.

Long-Term Objectives

Long-term objectives spring out of foresight, and it involves proper and adequate planning. It should be developed from a thorough understanding of the services offered. The long-term objectives should serve as a basic and/or foundation for strategy formulation. It is primarily based upon the internal information and external environment of the organization. The yardstick used for deter-mining the long-term objectives would be the direction the organization wants to take. In other words, what is the focus of this local church within this community? Once that focus is determined, long-term objectives that will enhance the focus can be identified and implemented.

To effectively determine the long-term objectives, it is best to have all available information that is critical to both external and internal environments of the organization or local church. The right information will always improve the changes of deciding on the appropriate long-term objectives that can propel the organization into a better future. It is best to keep in mind that the better the information, the better the chance for success. Long-term objectives should align with the mission and core values of the local church and must be suited to the internal situations and external environment of the organization.

The focus of strategy formulation should be the organizational improvement. The strategy formulation should be based on research and analysis. It should propose a detailed objective for performance improvement. It's best to highlight the present performance level at the local church, then explain the obstacles to improving performance that currently exist throughout the local church, and then identify the benefits to the organization that would result from the performance improvement. In the strategy formulation, the leadership team must propose metrics intended to be used to measure the implementation of the strategic plan and how those metrics align with the organization's mission and goals.

The implementation aspect of the strategic plan is critical for success. Thus, having formulated a strategy that is SMART, the focus should shift to effective implementation. One of the ways to ensure a better implementation strategy is to put in place performance scorecards. A performance scorecard is a set of business measures linked to mission strategies and goals that can be used to monitor and manage specific area of the organizational structure. Basically, scorecards include charts and graphs that are used to evaluate performance, monitor trends, identify strengths and weaknesses, and provide feedback on management actions.

For a scorecard to achieve its goal, there is a six-phase process that needs to be given careful attention during the developmental stage. The first phase involves collecting data that relates to or from the strategic goals of the organization, business objectives, and senior level measures. It includes identifying outcomes for teams, core work processes, as well as the expectations and requirements of all stakeholders. The second phase has to do with determining key results areas that are derived from the mission strategies and measures that are unique to the organization or, in this case, the local church. Some of the key areas to focus on would be financial success, community outreaches, loyalty to the church, manpower development, operational effectiveness, and community impact. The third phase is to cultivate. This phase focuses on refining the objectives and measures so as to become more relevant and result-oriented. This can be done by conducting a systematic review with the performance scorecard so as to monitor and improve performance. The fourth phase known as cascade is geared toward strengthening links, improving visibility on performance, and aligning every effort to meet the goal. This is the time work group scorecards are established and management scorecards are reviewed. Phase 5 is the connecting stage. This is done by developing individual performance plans that connect objectives and measures to individual staffs on the leader-ship team. The sixth phase is the confirming stage. This is the time to understand how measures on the scorecards are related to one another, with a goal of pulling them together so as to get the desired results.

Depending on the size of the congregation, you may not need elaborate software. Keep in mind that the goal of the performance scorecard is to provide a basic overview of how well you are doing and which areas need more focus. It would be really helpful if the scorecard focuses on measurable goals and clear ways to show outcomes. Below is an example of a simple performance scorecard.

STRATEGIC PLANNING

Scorecard Perspective	Objective	Measure	Target	Priority	Initiative	Data Source and Sharing	Data Owner
Financial	Budget vs. Baseline	Operate within allocated budget	+/- 10%	High	Tracking system for all revenue & expenses	Weekly budget reports & review	Project Manager & Budget Director
Attendance	Increase frequency	Community outreaches	5% variance monthly	High	Volunteering at schools and community events	Emails Memos Minutes of meetings	Department Heads
Membership	Increase awareness & the need to be connected	Teachings Discovery Dinners Cell groups	10%-15% new members	High	System to follow up; Monthly discovery dinner; Monitoring of cell groups attendance	Visitor Information; Insights from discovery dinners; Cell group reports	Hospitality committee; Leadership Team Lead Pastor
Workforce	Maintain qualified staff	Incentives; Staff engagement	2%-4% annual increase	High	Performance based recognitions;	Memos, emails, Newsletters	Lead Pastors, Board Chairs

The basic idea is that you should be able to decide on what the team wants the scorecard to do. What are the performance indicators? What are the key questions that need to be asked? Once the team has decided what the scorecard would achieve, put in useful data, measurable goals, and clear ways to show outcomes. Remember the performance scorecard should be used as a communication tool to educate the various departments of the church as to the direction and scope of the vision of the local church.

Using the performance scorecards will enhance effective and successful management of the strategic plan because it focuses on measures that matter to all stake-holders. More importantly, it supports the deployment of business strategies, provides visibility on process problems, and helps ensure that strategic goals or long term objectives of the organization are met. The performance scorecards if implemented would foster the relevancy of the local church within the community that the church exists. By adopting the performance scorecard, the local church would be able to link its long-term objectives to the critical success factors. The scorecard could be used in evaluating whether or not services offered are truly meeting the expectations of the mission. The scorecard would enhance the mission of the local church because it provides the leadership team with a tool to effectively monitor trends, identify strengths and weaknesses, and provide feedback for continuous improvement.

Another reason the performance scorecard is needed is that it would lead the organization more toward a system-thinking approach in that it links measures with organizational strategic goals, vision, and mission. The strategies utilized to measure and improve performance in a systems thinking environment is first and foremost, avoiding the tendency to focus on the isolated part of the system. Because the emphasis is on the whole, system-thinking approach explores solutions, ideas, and conclusions that are completely different from those generated by traditional linear or scientific management approaches. It "creates opportunities to learn more about the intricacies of the web, to study patterns and relationships among sub-systems, and to identify actions with the highest potential for positive sustainable change and continuous improvement" (Minarik et al. 2003, 4).

The performance scorecard would help the local church identify obstacles to improving performance that currently exist within the organization. Once again, I will use the Kingdom Harvest Ministries Inc., Liberia, West Africa, as an example. Between 1999 and 2006, the obstacle for improving performance as it relates to the core values, vision, and missions of the organization was inadequate departmental interaction due to poor communication. Despite every effort to solve the problem, the lack of a performance scorecard made it difficult for us to put in place a system to alleviate the so-called communication issue. Secondly, when an error is made, the system is not evaluated but the individual is blamed and reprimanded. What the leadership of KHM at that time failed to realize is that system thinking entails changes in practices as well as philosophy not on an individual basis (Selber 1998). The emphasis of system thinking is on "formulating a strategy that is aligned and integrated into a holistic framework to support breakthrough improvement" (Amelsberg 2002, 3).

There are many benefits that could result from the usage of the performance scorecards. Primarily, the score-cards would link or connect the organizational strategy to top-level goals or critical success factors. The scorecard can provide results-oriented feedback that enables the leadership teams to focus time, attention, and resources on improved results. Since systems thinking can lead to the intentional design of more effective management system which focuses on making the organizations "more capable of fulfilling their purpose" (Steele 2003, 5), the performance scorecards would lead to the creation of an intentional design that could lead to better decisions, thereby eliminating waste and achieving maximum results.

The impact of the performance scorecards is that measures would be provided that allows everyone to be focused. By using the scorecards as an implementation tool, the leadership team would be able to clarify out-comes, improve visibility of the processes, and eliminate the time and expense of tracking irrelevant information.

The performance scorecard can help the local church embrace system thinking. System thinking requires analysis from a broader perspective. It can be described as a framework for seeing patterns and interrelation-ships because it focuses on "the interactions rather than the part, the assumptions rather than the forecasts, and synthesis rather than analysis" (Steele, 2003. p.5). The strategies utilized to measure and improve performance in a systems thinking environment is first and foremost, avoiding the tendency to focus on the isolated part of the system. Because the emphasis is on the whole, system-thinking approach explores solutions, ideas, and conclusions that are completely different from those generated by traditional linear or scientific management approaches.

It is important to emphasize here that the performance scorecards will not work by copying from another organization. To reap its full benefits and experience its impacts, it must be developed to the unique needs and mission strategies of the organization or local church. If properly developed and implemented, the performance scorecards can enhance effective and successful management of any organization by focusing on measures that matter to all stakeholders.

CHAPTER SEVEN

DEVELOPING A WINNING STRATEGIC PLAN

The Influence of Organizational Culture on Developing a Strategic Plan

Organizational culture can influence the ultimate development and success of a strategic plan based upon the core values, goals, and mission of the organization or local church. Organizational culture usually springs out of the values and vision of the senior pastor as well as the history of the organization. As such, the culture defines the mission of the organization and set the tune for strategies and goals. Thus understanding the culture of an organization is paramount to the development and successful implementation of any strategic plan because effective organizations have strong, clear cultures that are consistent with their strategies.

The organizational culture dictates the nature of the strategic plan and defines its scope. External resources are evaluated and selected if their values are in alignment with that of the organizational culture. Prioritization of projects is link to the mission strategies of the local church, which springs from the organizational culture. Thus, a culture that does not embrace change but promotes autocratic and authoritative leadership over and above teamwork and does not value collective efforts can lead to disaster. Lack of trust can prevail in a culture that does not stress effective communication and accountability. On the other hand, if the organizational culture fosters collaboration and teamwork and encourages people to do what needs to be done by consciously incorporating conditions that facilitate innovation and achievement, projects are completed in a timely manner with fewer setbacks (Back 2004).

The Role of the Senior Pastor in the Development of the Strategic Plan

Considering the role of the senior pastor, it is vital to understand that the senior pastor has the potential to either make or break the growth strategy of the local church. For the strategic plan to be successful, the senior pastor should be able to foster innovation, be growth oriented, thorough, persistent, discrete, persuasive, and comfortable with change. More importantly, the senior pastor must be able to work through existing networks to uncover opportunities, build coalitions, and make change happen. The senior pastor should be able to establish vision and direction for the strategic plan. By so doing, he/ she can define the priorities of the strategic plan, as well as guide and motivate the team members and stakeholders. Building coalition should be the priority of the senior pastor as it has the potential to enhance his/her role. By building coalition, the senior pastor, through consultation and collaboration, can build the morale of the team as each person would feel his/her import is important.

It is important for the senior pastor to explore how the organizational culture of the local church and human behavior could possibly influence either negatively or positively the successful development and implementation of the strategic plan. Once the influence of the organizational culture is understood, it is the responsibility of the senior pastor to effectively communicate the direction of the strategic plan while it is in the development process. Ground rules should be established, expectations made cleared, and goals clearly defined and aligned with the mission of the organization or local church.

In order to develop a winning strategic plan, the senior pastor must be comfortable with change, be clear on direction, be thorough, encourage a participative management style, and be persuasive, persistent, and discrete. By being comfortable with change, the senior pastor can build confidence in the process as all issues of uncertainty will be clarified. Such confidence can empower everyone involved with the process of developing the strategic plan to see potential problems as opportunities. With a clear goal of what to do and how to do it, everyone involved can eventually view potential setbacks as "temporary blips in an otherwise straight path to a goal" (Kanter 2004, 155). By being persuasive, persistent, and discrete, the senior pastor can instill in the membership a sense of being realistic about the strategic plan. The members will under-stand that they cannot achieve their goals overnight, but by perseverance and tactfulness, they can meet deadlines and complete the strategic plan on time.

Challenges in Developing a Winning Strategic Plan

There are many challenges that face any strategist. Yet there are two that I think are the most challenging to the leadership of the local church as it relates to planning with the goal of making the local church more relevant within the community. The first challenge is gathering the right information to aid in the process of developing the strategic plan. Conducting an effective external and internal environmental analysis is not an easy task. There are a lot of data to go through and to integrate. A better under-standing and analysis of these data serves as the basic for conducting a better SWOT analysis, matched pair analysis, and/or a grand strategy clusters analysis (all of which will be discussed in this chapter). The second challenge would be properly using the diverse inputs or expert opinions of the planning team members when they are not in agreement. There will be times when either the pastoral staffs or another member of the team will make a choice or decision that someone would be in disagreement with. Properly collaborating diverse opinions often requires critical thinking skills. There will be times, trust me, when it would be difficult to clearly agree upon which view to incorporate into the process. However, by paying much attention to the information gathered, the best decisions will be made.

Principles to Consider in Developing the Strategic Plan

There are five principles that the local church leadership team must carefully consider when developing a strategic plan.

1. A good strategy springs out of foresights, proper planning, and setting of long-term goals. Long-term goals or objectives enable an organization to define its growth parameters and target market for a period of five years. The yardstick used for determining the long-term objectives would be the direction the

organization wants to take. In other words, what is the primary focus of the local church within the community? Once that focus is deter-mined, long-term objectives that will enhance the focus can be identified and implemented. To effectively determine the long-term objectives, it is best to have all available information that is critical to both external and internal environments of the organization or local church. The right information will always improve the chances of deciding on the appropriate long-term objectives that can propel the local church into a better future. The better the information, the better the chance for success. It is important to understand that the long-term objective serves as a basic to the strategy formulation of the organization. As such, the long-term objectives should align with the mission and core values of the local church and must be suited to the internal situations and external environment of the local church.

2. SWOT and matched pair analysis are important. After the long-term objectives have been identified, the next step is to identify the strategy of implementation. The first approach would be to conduct a SWOT analysis. The SWOT analysis identifies the internal strengths and weaknesses of the organization as well as the external opportunities and threats facing the organization. The next step would be to perform a matched pair analysis for more strategic options or alternatives. A matched pair analysis is the best tool in determining the strategy of implementation for the long-term objectives established. A matched pair analysis extends the scope of the traditional SWOT analysis by matching the internal strengths

and weaknesses of the organization to its external opportunities and threats thereby enabling more strategic alternatives.

3. A grand strategy must be developed. A grand strategy is intended to give the local church direction in securing an advantage within the community.

4. To become successful in developing a grand strategy that will launch the local church into securing an advantage, the leadership of the local church must understand the high and low of the community in which the church exists and the high and low of the local church's outreach efforts within the community. It is important to use a grand strategy clusters matrix in developing the grand strategy for an organization. Depending on the trends within the domicile of the local church, the grand strategy will serve as a proactive strategic response that can help the local church improves its advantage. The grand strategy cluster matrix takes into consideration three important facts. The SWOT analysis which focuses on the internal strengths and weaknesses as well as the external opportunities and threats faced by the organization, the financial analysis which includes forecast and actual, and the domicile analysis/reports, which shows trends within the community. By using the grand strategy clusters matrix, the leadership team can effectively identify the local church's position and recommend a strategic response that will enable the organization to achieve its goal. The objective is to decide on a strategic alternative that will secure the organization's position and enable the retention of its position.

STRATEGIC PLANNING

5. Develop a strategic road map. A strategic road map is intended to help an organization align its strategies with the vision and long-term objectives.

6. The strategic roadmap helps organizations to set milestones that will enable them realize their vision. The road map helps an organization defines its strategic alternatives and corresponding goals that will enhance the realization of its vision. The roadmap also defines the strategic initiatives the organization has to undertake in other to consolidate its position within the community. The first step in developing a strategic roadmap is to identify the strategic alternatives. The second step is to determine or define the goals that will lead to the successful implementation of the strategies identified. For example, if the goal is to raise up vibrant believers who know, honor, and fear God, thereby transforming and impacting the community as champions and leaders (Kingdom Harvest Ministries Inc. Mission statement), there would be a need to decide on a structure that can effectively propel the local church into achieving such goal.

7. Critical to the successful attainment of an organization's vision is an effective and well-implemented strategy. A strategy that is well developed and properly implemented can position an organization to launch successfully into its future. To effectively define an organization's strategic initiatives, it is best to use the SWOT analysis as a guide. This will ensure that the strategic initiatives are relevant to trends within the community as well as situations within the organization or local church.

As stated in chapter 6, for a strategy to become effective, it should meet two requirements—first, the strategic plan should be aligned with the vision of the local church. In developing the strategic plan, the leadership should ensure that the long-term objectives are aligned with the mission and core values of the organization. Research should be conducted on both the external and internal environments so as to make sure the long-term objectives are suited to the internal situations and external environment of the organization. This is important because the long-term objectives should serve as a basic to the strategy formulation of the organization. Second, the strategic plan should have a well-developed implementation strategy that has SMART objectives. Once long-term objectives are identified, leadership should follow through to make sure that the implementation strategy is SMART. This can be done by asking the following questions. Are the objectives of this implementation strategy simple enough for everyone to grasp? Are the objectives motivational enough to move everyone to action? Are the objectives agreeable and attainable within the timeframe? Are the objectives realistic enough to achieve the desired results? And are the objectives properly time frame or have the proper time limits to ensure adequate implementation?

Remember a practical long-term objective should define the growth parameter of the local church for a period of five years. The best determining factor for an effective implementation strategy is conducting a SWOT and matched pair analysis. For the internal and external environment, it would be best practice to conduct a SWOT analysis and later a matched pair analysis because the goal is to have more strategic options or alternatives for effectively implementing the strategies developed.

Understanding the Grand Strategy Clusters

A grand strategy clusters is important to the development of a winning strategic plan. It is important to remember that the grand strategy will serve as a proactive strategic response that can help the local church improves its advantage. The Grand Strategy Cluster matrix takes into consideration three important facts. The SWOT analysis which focuses on the internal strengths and weaknesses as well as the external opportunities and threats faced by the organization, the financial analysis which includes forecast and actual, and the domicile analysis/reports which shows trends within the community. By using the grand strategy clusters matrix, the leadership team can effectively identify the local church's position and recommend a strategic response that will enable the organization to achieve its goal. The objective is to decide on a strategic alternative that will secure the organization's position and enable the retention of its position. If you must have a winning strategic plan that will make the local church relevant within your community, please do not overlook or neglect any of the analysis the grand strategy clusters is intended to address. Make sure to conduct a SWOT analysis, financial analysis, and domicile analysis. Using these tools in the grand strategy clusters will improve all options in the preparing of the strategic plan of the organization.

The Importance of Developing a Strategic Road Map

A strategic road map does four things: It helps an organization align its strategies with the vision and long-term objectives. It helps organizations set milestones that will enable them realize their vision. It helps an organization defines its strategic alternatives and corresponding goals that will enhance the realization of its vision. And it defines the strategic initiatives the organization has to undertake in other to consolidate its position within the community. In developing the strategic plan for the local church, it is important to use the roadmap as an implementation strategy. By using the road map as an implementation strategy, the leadership can be certain that the strategies are aligned with the vision of the local church. Another reason the road map should be used as an implementation strategy is that it allows the leadership to set milestones that can aid in the implementation of the vision as well as define strategic alternatives and define the strategic initiatives the organization has to undertake in other to consolidate its position within the community.

Developing Kingdom Harvest Ministries Inc. Liberia Strategic Plan

This information provided below is intended to serve two purposes: be an illustrative example of how Kingdom Harvest Ministries in Liberia emerged from stagnation (after direction was lost as stated in chapter two) into a strategic organization that is making maximum impact for the glory of God through strategic planning and serve as a model to any local church that is serious about impacting the community in which ministries exist.

The Kingdom Harvest Ministries Inc., Liberia, West Africa, is governed by an Ecclesiastical Council comprising of clergies, elders, and laymen for consulting, advising, and deciding upon matters of the ministries. The ministries consists of three distinct principal organs: general council, executive council, and ministerial council. The general council is the highest decision-making body with the executive council as the administrative body. The ministerial council deals with all issues affecting the clergy while the executive council coordinates the affairs of all other entities through a secretariat. From July 1999 when the ministry was launched to July 2005, Kingdom Harvest Ministries Inc. has never had a consolidated strategic plan although it has a plan on how churches are to be established that is outlined in the Church Planting Manual.

After many setbacks and realizing that critical to the successful attainment of an organization's vision is an effective and well-implemented strategy, we decided that during the 2005 convention, which also marks the sixth anniversary of the KHM, that a strategic plan be developed in which the long-term objectives are properly aligned with the mission and core values of the ministries. We acknowledge the fact that a strategy that is well developed and properly implemented can position an organization to launch successfully into its future. Accordingly, a detailed and consolidated corporate plan was developed to guide the ministries from 2005 to 2010. A strategic planning workshop was organized to educate all stakeholders to the importance and necessity of developing a strategic plan. In addition, further information was obtained from stakeholders by a series of interviews as well as a critical and analytical review of the ministries activities in the first five years of operations.

The Strategic plan was intended to set the frame-work from which every sector of the ministries can be guided with respect to the strategic objectives of KHM. Every stakeholder understood that the strategic plan when developed is intended to become an integral part of all decision making processes and should be referred to whenever a decision affecting KHM is made. One of my roles as the visionary was to ensure that the strategic plan provides a clear indication of the direction KHM is to take in the next five years. Since the plan was the first for KHM, as the visionary, I made it clear to every leader that the strategic plan should be revisited and updated when-ever necessary due to fundamental shifts in policy and/or significant change in the driving forces that affect the structure and processes of the organization. As the visionary, I also ensured that the strategic plan was the culmination of consensus discussions of stakeholders focusing on KHM's challenges to best position the ministries in fulfilling its vision and mission. The objective of the strategic plan was to be a key tool in providing direction to the leadership of the secretariat and the pastoral staff of each local church.

As the visionary, it was my responsibility to make sure everyone understood the key direction points such as the vision, mission statement, critical success factors, strategic objectives, and strategic objectives action plans. It was made clear that the strategic plan be used as a decision-making tool and become a working document that will be reviewed at board meetings, with periodic briefings on progress and specific action plans.

As a local pastor and/or denominational leader reader this book, it is important to remember that organizational culture can influence the ultimate development and success of a strategic plan based upon the core values, goals, and mission of the organization or local church. Organizational culture usually springs out of the values and vision of the senior pastor as well as the history of the organization. In developing the strategic plan of KHM in 2005, as the visionary, I had to ensure that everyone understood the values and vision of the ministry. Keep in mind that one of the roles of the senior pastor in the development of a strategic plan is to be thorough, persistent, persuasive, and comfortable with change.

The first thing I did was to conduct a survey to determine how many leaders and members of the organization actually

STRATEGIC PLANNING

knew and understood the vision and mission statement of the ministry. Based upon the data collected and the analysis thereof, it was decided to teach the vision and mission statement before moving ahead with the development of the strategic plan. The data analysis showed that about 33 percent of the entire leadership knew the vision and mission statement and only 12 percent could articulate same well. Only 5 percent of the entire member-ship had a clue as to what is the vision and mission of the organization. Based upon our findings through data mining, we knew that we could not develop a strategic plan without orientating everyone as to the values and vision. We had nothing to dictate the nature of the strategic plan and define its scope. By teaching the vision and mission statement of KHM before developing the strategic plan, every stakeholder understood that the vision and missions of KHM are designed to capture its direction and strategic focus. The vision and mission statement will serve to provide guidance for all stakeholders to effectively and efficiently achieve the set objectives of KHM. The vision of KHM as was originally written in 1999 when the ministry started is "to reap the end-time harvest while it is still ripe by means of strategic-level warfare." In 2001 (four years before the development of the first strategic plan), the vision was expanded as followed.

To reap the end-time harvest while it is still ripe by means of strategic level warfare:

- Providing spiritual supports through saturated church planting with a strong emphasis on discipleship.
- Providing educational supports with a strong biblical foundation by establishing schools where ever a church is planted.
- Providing medical supports by building health centers within every region of Liberia where the need exists the most.

The mission statement as written in 1999 when the ministry started is "to raise up a generation of vibrant believers who know, honor, and fear God thereby deeply impacting and transforming their communities as champions and leaders." In 2001, the mission statement was expanded as "to raise up a generation of vibrant believers who know, honor, and fear God thereby deeply impacting and transforming their communities as champions and leaders in order to fulfill our obligation to repossess our stolen spiritual heritage through strategic-level evangelism and discipleship."

As a result of teaching the vision and mission statement before developing the strategic plan, everyone agrees that the vision as an image of the future, is so compelling that it motivates individuals to action, is result-oriented, is clear and concise, adopts a consumer/stakeholder perspective, so that resistance to change declines, that it seeks to ensure that the KHM strategy is aligned with its working environment and the ministries' core competencies and that the vision will empower everyone to drive the process of change. One of the roles of the senior pastor as discussed earlier is to explore how the organizational culture of the local church and human behavior could possibly influence either negatively or positively the successful development and implementation of the strategic plan. Once the influence of the organizational culture is understood, it is the responsibility of the senior pastor to effectively communicate the direction of the strategic plan while it is in the development process. When people understand the culture of the organization, ground rules can be established without conflict, expectations can be made cleared, and goals can be clearly defined and aligned with the mission of the organization or local church.

Since all stakeholders now to a greater degree under-stood the organizational culture of KHM through get-ting a grape

STRATEGIC PLANNING

on the values and vision of the ministry, we were able to put together share values that everyone must adhere to in positioning the ministry to have an advantage within every community where ministry exists. After much deliberation, we decided that the following shared values will guide the general council, ministerial council, the secretariat and all members in our conduct with one another, and our external stakeholders as we relentlessly pursue the vision and mission of the KHM. A commitment to teamwork for higher productivity and efficiency, a commitment to professionalism in all that we do for and in the name of KHM; a commitment to protect and safeguard the assets of KHM at all times, a commitment to portray a positive, proactive, and value added image of the KHM at all times, a commitment to value integrity, truthfulness and authenticity and a commitment to treat one another with respect and dignity.

In developing a strategic plan, it is important that the senior pastor builds confidence in the process. By building confidence, everyone involved can be empowered to see potential problems as opportunities. What people need when developing a strategic plan is a clear goal of what to do and how to do it. To build confidence in the process, I also did another teaching entitled "Facing Our Challenges Strategically." I took my text from Nehemiah 4. I emphasized that facing KHM challenges strategically means we have to build both physical and spiritual walls at the same time. I told them that it is important to understand that we will face challenges for every task undertaken for the glory of God. I encouraged them by emphasizing that a willingness to work under any circumstance is essential to facing our challenges and that intercession must be a priority in the process of facing our challenges. I challenged them by stating that strategic planning ensures effectiveness in facing our challenges and that when we face our challenges strategically and successfully implement our strategic plans, we are bound to success in all our endeavors, no matter the odds.

Adapting the Five Principles of Strategic Planning into KHM Strategic Plan

The first principle of strategic planning is that a good strategy springs out of foresights, proper planning, and setting of long-term goals. In developing the first strategic plan for KHM, I started to conscientize all stakeholders between 2003 to 2005 as to what strategic planning is about and the need for us to develop one for the organization. We spent about a year in gathering data from July 2004 to July 2005. The process took a longer time because I was not residing in Liberia and almost all data collection was done remotely through either e-mail communications or telephone conversations. We had a weeklong intensive workshop and spent a whole day in completing and adapting the first strategic plan.

Long-term goals or objectives enable an organization to define its growth parameters. The yardstick used for determining the long-term objectives would be the direction the organization wants to take. In other words, what is the primary focus of the local church within the community? Once that focus is determined, long-term objectives that will enhance the focus can be identified and implemented. One of the process used in determining KHM's direction was the teaching of the values, vision, and missions as described above.

To ensure that everyone understood the direction of every KHM entity (churches, schools, clinics, and youth centers), I asked repeatedly during the workshop, "What is the primary mission of KHM in the communities we serve?" Keep in mind that the focus and emphasis of strategic management is not control or power but getting others motivated to positively contribute to the process. Motivating others to action and ownership through full participation could bring forth transformation in any organization and is a breeding ground for innovation. To enable a higher level of performance, strategic management proposes that friendly partnership and collaboration can be effective when leadership confirms the objective by asking and focusing on what is the purpose. How does it align with the team's goal? By confirming the objective, the strategic leader is establishing awareness and better understanding. As we confirmed the objective of KHM during the developmental stage of the strategic plan, we were able to establish and affirm a sense of identity for the organization and offer an appealing future vision. Conger (1999) suggests that without a strategic plan, no organization can develop a deep collective identity that heightens both individual and collective self-efficacy. Now that the collective identity was heightens, it was suggested that we develop a statement to be known as KHM Affirmation of Faith. The affirmation of faith, which is an expanded version of the mission and vision of KHM, is recited in every service held in any KHM church. Our purpose was not to develop an affirmation of faith but the confirming of the objective created excitement and innovative thinking. The KHM affirmation is as followed:

> We affirm by the power of the Holy Spirit that we are being raised up by the Lord Jesus Christ to reap the end time harvest while it is still ripe. We are being empowered to burst through the enemy's zone and set the captives free from the clutches of Satan transforming them into vibrant believers who

know, honor, and fear God and can deeply impact and transform their communities as champions and leaders.

Now that every stakeholder understood the direction of KHM, developing the long-term objectives was not difficult. Since it is best to have all available information that is critical to both external and internal environments of the organization as a means of effectively determining the long-term objectives, we did not leave out any piece of information, no matter how insignificant in our estimation. The right information will always improve the chances of deciding on the appropriate long-term objectives that can propel the local church into a better future. It is always good to keep in mind that the better the information, the better the chance for success. It is important to understand that the long-term objective serves as a basic to the strategy formulation of the organization. As such, the long-term objectives should align with the mission and core values of the local church and must be suited to the internal situations and external environment of the local church. After considering all relevant information as it relates to KHM's internal and external environments, as well as the mission and core values of the organization, we concluded on the following long-term objectives.

1. KHM is and will continue to be a *church-planting movement* that will plant churches and establish schools within every region of Liberia in fulfillment of its mandate to prepare each generation to know, honor, and fear God.
2. KHM shall continue to be an autonomous, self-financing, self-propagating body.

STRATEGIC PLANNING

3. Politically, KHM shall hold no partisan allegiance to any political party so that the influence of the gospel to reach *all* will not be compromised.
4. To reap the end-time harvest while it is still ripe by means of strategic-level evangelism as outlined in the church-planting manual.
5. To operate KHM under sound financial management.
6. To plant in the next five years (2005–2010) ten churches and establish two academy schools.

After the long-term objectives have been identified, the next step is to identify the strategy of implementation, which is principle number 2 of strategic planning. The first approach is conducting a SWOT (strengths, weaknesses, opportunities, and threats) analysis. The SWOT analysis identifies the internal strengths and weaknesses of the organization as well as the external opportunities and threats facing the organization. Our SWOT analysis was based upon data collected for over a year. Data-based problem identification is an important method because it can "be used to clarify a problem, to establish a baseline, and to measure the efficacy of interventions" (Burns 2004, 64). Data mining is essential to strategic management because data can help with the assessment and diagnosis process. The data we collected was used to properly clarify and analyze problems, as well as enhance the process of effectively exploring and selecting the best interventions.

Based upon our internal analysis, we were able to identify our strengths and weaknesses. For strengths, we had a united, committed, and skilled workforce. There were regular and consistent trainings. There has being a strong emphasis on keeping the vision in focus. Good accountability and stewardship was practiced. Leadership at the local levels was good. To a greater degree, we had not abundant but adequate resources to help advance the work, and we were making use of technology. For weaknesses, the means of communications and information dissemination were unreliable and unstable. We lacked strong, coordinated leadership at the national level (i.e., the secretariat). There was a lack of timely funding though often adequate to meet some needs. There had been ineffective distribution of resources to enhance and speedily implement the vision.

Based upon the external analysis, we were able to identify our opportunities and threats based upon current trends within our external environment. For opportunities, we realized that now was the best time for property acquisition as the cost is very reasonable because the nation is just emerging out of sixteen years of civil war. We also felt we had a better chance of investing is farmlands and farming equipments for self sustainability. Another opportunity we saw was the need for sports ministry to reach the many young and former combatants who had nothing to do and were all eager to participate in sporting activities. There was also an opportunity to reach many through feeding programs for children who are less fortunate as we emerged out of war. Since many homes were destroyed and many are still displaced from the residence locations, it would be great if we could establish old folks homes as many people lost their homes and do not have much room to cater efficiently to their old folks. For threats, we identified three major areas. The lack of attractive salary to maintain qualified personnel, the lack of social activities to keep the young people engaged and continuously involved, and economic uncertainty as the ministry was primarily supported out of my pocket and donations from friends I have here in the USA. What would happen if I lost either of my jobs in the USA or my friends could not afford to help regularly? As you can see, our external

STRATEGIC PLANNING

analysis was not limited to Liberia. Since I am residing in the USA, we had to include trends here in the USA so as to properly prepare for the worse situation.

The following diagrams are the actual SWOT and matched pair analysis of Kingdom Harvest Ministries Inc. Liberia.

Having completed our SWOT analysis, the next step was to perform a matched pair analysis and grand strategy cluster for more strategic options or alternatives. A matched pair analysis is the best tool in determining the strategy of implementation for the long-term objectives established. A matched pair analysis extends the scope of the traditional SWOT analysis by matching the internal strengths and weaknesses of the organization to its external opportunities and threats thereby enabling more strategic alternatives.

KHM 2007 Matched Pair Analysis

Strength/Opportunities	Strength/Weaknesses	Strength/Threats
Strength: Adequate Resources to help advance the work **Opportunity:** Investment is farm lands and farming equipments.	**Strength:** Evolving good leadership at the local level **Weakness:** Lack of strong coordinated leadership at the national level.	**Strength:** United, committed and skilled work force. **T:** Lack of attractive salary to maintain qualified staffs
Opportunities/Weaknesses	**Opportunities/Threats**	**Weaknesses/Threats**
O: Property acquisition as the cost at this time is very reasonable. **W:** Lack of timely funding though often adequate to meet some needs.	**O:** Sports ministry to reach the many young and former combatants. **T:** Lack of social activities to keep the young people.	**W:** Lack of timely funding though often adequate to meet some needs. **T:** Lack of attractive salary to maintain qualified staffs
Strengths/Oppor/Weaknesses	**Strengths/Oppor/Threats**	**Oppor/Weaknesses/Threats**
S: Strong emphasis on keeping the vision in focus. **O:** Sports ministry to reach the many young and former combatants. **W:** Ineffective distribution of resources to enhance and speedily implement the vision.	**S:** Good accountability and stewardship **O:** Property acquisition as the cost at this time is very reasonable. **T:** Economic uncertainty.	**O:** Sports ministry to reach the many young and former combatants. **W:** unstable communications and information dissemination **T:** Lack of attractive salary to maintain qualified staffs

The above matched pair analysis gives Kingdom Harvest Ministries in Liberia a better picture in determining the strategy of implementation for the long-term objectives established. By conducting a matched pair analysis, the local church can adapt a systems thinking approach as a means of aligning the mission with the long-term objectives identified. The matched pair analysis can improve performance because it avoids the tendency to focus on the isolated part of the system. When planning and thinking strategically, the emphasis should be on the whole, thereby exploring solutions, ideas, and conclusions that are completely different from those generated by traditional linear or scientific management approaches. Minarik et al. (2003) state that systems thinking approach "creates opportunities to learn more about the intricacies of the web, to study pat-terns and relationships among subsystems, and to identify actions with the highest potential for positive sustainable change and continuous improvement" (p. 4).

Interpreting the Matched Pair Analysis of KHM

The interpretation of a matched pair analysis is important for effective control and evaluation of the organization strategic initiatives. The interpretation will help the organization see patterns that can help in the process of identifying strategic alternatives. The interpretation can also help the organization to come with better ideas, solutions, and conclusions. The analysis reveals that most of the times KHM has adequate resources to help advance the work as compared to other churches in Liberia. Based upon the matched pair analysis, we saw that the opportunity of investment in farm lands and farming equipments would be the best use of our resources. This idea based upon the interpretation of the matched pair analysis is aligned with our long term goal #2 which is KHM shall continue to be an autonomous, self-financing, self-propagating body.

When our strengths and weaknesses were matched, the analysis reveals that we have a critical problem with leadership. While there is a strong evolving leadership at the local church and entity levels, the ministries as a whole lacks strong, coordinated leadership at the national level. As for our strengths and threats, the analysis reveals that while it is true that we have a united, committed, and skilled work-force, the ministry lacks attractive salary to maintain the qualified staffs we have at the various entities. When the opportunities were matched with the weaknesses, the analysis reveals that while property acquisition would be a good investment because of the low cost due to the country just emerging out of war, the ministry often lacks timely funding though we always have fund to meet some needs.

For opportunity and threats, the analysis reveals that we need to focus and enhance our sports ministry at the various churches and schools as a means of reaching the young people and former combatants because the whole nation lacks strong social activities to keep the young people motivated and engaged. For weaknesses and threats, the analysis reveals that unless we act quickly and proactively, the lack of timely funding would make it difficult for the ministry to put in place a competitive and better salary structure to keep the qualified and committed staffs we now have as they might seek out better employment to cater to the needs of their families. An example of this analysis is my brother who was afraid to take outside employment for a while because of his commitment to the vision. After much encouragement from me (although I was worried as to who would fill his position as the chief administrator at the high school), he took a job that is paying him 300 percent more than what we could afford to offer him. Since my brother left, the ministry has lost five other persons. Though they got outside employment, the churches are benefiting from their tithes, offerings, and often donations to projects. The matched pair analysis in the areas of weaknesses and threats helped us to strategize as to how to create a better incentive package to maintain the best of talents available to us as a ministry.

As we matched the strengths, opportunities, and weaknesses, the analysis reveals that the strong emphasis on keeping the vision in focus would help us reach many young people, but we have to address the problem of ineffective distribution of resources to enhance and speedily implement the vision. As for the strengths, opportunities, and threats, the analysis reveals that because we have good accountability and stewardship especially at the high school, we must apply every effort for property acquisition as the cost at this time is very reasonable due to the economic uncertainty that is prevailing in the nation as a result of the just ended civil war and the worldwide economic recession. When we matched the opportunities with the weaknesses and threats, the analysis reveals that while there is a greater opportunity for us to reach many young people through sports ministry, our problem of unstable communications and information dissemination coupled with the threat of losing qualified staffs due to the lack of attractive salary could seriously hinder the process. The goal of performing the matched pair analysis is formulating a strategy that is aligned with the vision and integrated into a holistic framework to support improvement and better coordination. The matched pair analysis will helped enable the local church to link its mission strategies and goals as well as monitor trends, manage and evaluate performance, identify strengths and weaknesses, and provide feedback on actions that are required.

STRATEGIC PLANNING

The Grand Strategy Cluster Matrix

The grand strategy cluster matrix takes into consideration three important facts. The SWOT analysis that focuses on the internal strengths and weaknesses as well as the external opportunities and threats faced by the organization, the financial analysis which includes forecast and actual, and the domicile analysis/reports which shows trends within the community. By using the grand strategy clusters matrix, we were able to effectively identify KHM's position and recommend a strategic response that will enable the organization to achieve its goal. The objective is to decide on a strategic alternative that will secure the organization's position and enable the retention of its position. Having completed the grand strategy, we came up with strategic alternatives that we deemed as critical success factors. Understanding out critical success factors would help us to improve operations, take on additional responsibilities, and consider the extent to which we focus on issues. Below are the critical success factors based upon the matched pair analysis and grand strategy cluster.

KHM will continue to be a church-planting movement that will plant churches and establish schools within every region of Liberia in fulfillment of the mandate to prepare our generation to know, honor, and fear God. As such, we must promote good leadership at all levels to enhance trust, transparency, and integrity. Good and effective leadership often lead to quality, trustworthy ministry. We must focus on the retention of highly qualified and motivated workforce. The retention of suitably qualified personnel is central to our ability to carrying out the core vision. It is important that we operate KHM under sound financial management. To have sound financial management, we must ensure we keep our balance sheet low geared to attract adequate funding for continued operations and future investment.

We should maintain our partnership with US-based churches but keep our focus on local initiates for the sustenance of the work in Liberia. US-based funding should be seen as short-term. If the work in Liberia is to be properly sustained, we must support the work locally. We must continue to be an autonomous, self-financing, self-propagating body. Politically, the ministry as a body shall hold no partisan allegiance to any political party so that the influence of the gospel to reach *all* will not be compromised.

In fulfilling the great commission of our Lord Jesus Christ, it is imperative that we reach everyone regardless of political persuasion. As a ministry, we will not promote any one political party. We must enforce effective communication at all levels of the ministries because the lack of communication often leads to misunderstood directions and misplaced priorities. We must constantly strive to bridge the generational gap and speedily advance the gospel through the use of technology. The secretariat must ensure that we properly distribute resources to enhance the work because dissatisfaction is a breeding ground for lack of progress. Every effort must be applied to minimize dissatisfaction.

The strategic alternatives developed based upon our long-term objectives will help us produce the right culture and create an atmosphere of ownership where inputs are solicited and valued on all levels of the organization. The strategic alternatives are critical success factors because they enable us set benchmarks along with short- and long-term goals that are measurable and can lead to proficiency.

The diagram below details how SWOT analysis, critical success factors, and strategic objectives are linked. The diagram is intended to show a pattern in how the organization or local church intends to meet its critical success factors and strategic objectives.

STRATEGIC PLANNING

SWOT Analysis Strengths:	Critical success factors	Long-term objectives affected (number)
United, committed and skilled work force.	Retention of highly qualified and motivated work force	Numbers 1-6
Strong emphasis on keeping the vision in focus.	Continue to be a church-planting movement in fulfillment of the mandate to prepare our generation to know, honor, and fear God.	Numbers 1-6
Regular and consistent trainings.	Retention of highly qualified and motivated work force	Numbers 1, 4, 6
Good accountability and stewardship	Operate KHM under sound financial management.	Numbers 1, 2, 5
Evolving good leadership at the local level	Promote good leadership at all levels to enhance trust, transparency, and integrity.	Numbers 1-6
Adequate Resources to help advance the work	Properly distribute resources to enhance the work	Numbers 1-6
The use of technology.	Bridge the generational gap and speedily advance the gospel	Numbers 1-6

SWOT Analysis Weaknesses:	Critical success factors	Long-term objectives affected (number)
Lack of timely funding.	Operate KHM under sound financial management.	Number 5
Unstable communications and information dissemination	Enforce effective communication at all levels of the Ministries	Numbers 1-6
Ineffective distribution of resources to enhance and speedily implement the vision.	Properly distribute resources to enhance the work	Numbers 1-6
Lack of strong coordinated leadership on the national level.	Promote good leadership at all levels to enhance trust, transparency, and integrity.	Numbers 1-6

SWOT Analysis Opportunities:	Critical success factors	Long-term objectives affected (number)
Property acquisition as the cost at this time is very reasonable.	Properly distribute resources to enhance the work	Numbers 1, 4, 5
Investment is farm lands and farming equipments.	Maintain our partnership with US-based churches but keep our focus on local initiates for the sustenance of the work in Liberia	Numbers 1-6
Sports ministry to reach the many young and former combatants.	Bridge the generational gap and speedily advance the gospel	Numbers 1-6
The use of technology.	Bridge the generational gap and speedily advance the gospel	Numbers 1, 5, 6
Feeding programs for children who are less fortunate as we emerge out of war.	Properly distribute resources to enhance the work	Numbers 1, 5, 6
Establishing of old folks homes as many people lost their homes and do not have much room to cater efficiently to their old folks.	Promote good leadership at all levels to enhance trust, transparency, and integrity.	Numbers 1-6

SWOT Analysis Threats:	Critical success factors	Long-term objectives affected (number)
Lack of attractive salary to maintain qualified staffs	Retention of highly qualified and motivated work force	Numbers 1-6
Lack of social activities to keep the young people.	Bridge the generational gap and speedily advance the gospel	Numbers 1-4
Lack of transportation to travel outside of Monrovia.	Properly distribute resources to enhance the work	Numbers 1, 4, 5, 6
Economic uncertainty	Operate KHM under sound financial management	Number 5

The numbers under long-term objectives affected are in reference to the long-term objectives already established and earlier stated in this chapter. However, for the sake of clarity and easy reference for anyone who might want to use this as a guide, KHM long term objectives are stated again below.

1. KHM is and will continue to be a *church-planting movement* that will plant churches and establish schools within every region of Liberia in fulfillment of its

mandate to prepare each generation to know, honor, and fear God.
2. KHM shall continue to be an autonomous, self-financing, self-propagating body.
3. Politically, KHM shall hold no partisan allegiance to any political party, so that the influence of the gospel to reach *all* will not be compromised;
4. To reap the end-time harvest while it is still ripe by means of strategic-level evangelism as outlined in the *church-planting manual*.
5. To operate KHM under sound financial management.
6. To plant in the next five years (2005–2010) ten churches and establish two academy schools.

KHM's Strategic Road Map

A strategic road map does four things. It helps an organization align its strategies with the vision and long-term objectives. It helps organizations set milestones that will enable them realize their vision. It helps an organization defines its strategic alternatives and corresponding goals that will enhance the realization of its vision. And it defines the strategic initiatives the organization has to undertake in other to consolidate its position within the community. After we have developed the strategic plan for Kingdom Harvest Ministries, we used the road map as our implementation strategy. By using the road-map as an implementation strategy, we are certain that the strategies are aligned with the vision of the ministry. The road map as an implementation strategy allows us to set milestones that can aid in the implementation of the vision as well as define the strategic initiatives we have to undertake in other to consolidate our position within the community. Since the development of the strategic plan in 2005, we had revised and updated the strategic road map twice, in 2007 and 2008. Below is an exert from the actual 2008 revised road map. The actual road map is done in PowerPoint with a slightly different format than presented below.

Revised KHM Strategic Road Map for 2009-2010

Strategy # 1: Establish 10 churches by 2010
KHM would have established 7 churches by the end of 2008. We would be left with 3 more churches and 2 more years to reach our church planting goal for the time indicated.
The goal:
Trained Man power as leaders for the churches to ensure a healthy disciple-making church.
Actions required to meet strategic plan # 1
1. Operate School of Missions (a short term, customized church planting and discipleship training for man power development)
A. **What are the strategic initiatives?** Create criteria for those who should attend the school of missions. Urge local pastors to spot potential gifting and calling. Find and train leaders on the field. Operate two School of Missions on the DuPort Rd at Mountain of Praise and at Praise Sanctuary, the headquarters church.
B. **Accountability (who is responsible):** The Senior Pastors of Praise Sanctuary and Mountain of Praise
C. **Milestones/Indicators**: Identify potential calling & recruit for the SOM. Develop curriculum for the school of mission by 08/25/08. Start the SOM by 08/30/08.
D. **Time frame:** 1st session 08/30/08 to 10/31/08. Visitation of new areas for church planting every Saturday with students

Strategy # 1: Establish 10 churches by 2010
KHM would have established 7 churches by the end of 2008. We would be left with 3 more churches and 2 more years to reach our church planting goal for the time indicated.
The goal:
Trained Man power as leaders for the churches to ensure a healthy disciple-making church.
Actions required to meet strategic plan # 1
Appoint a Field Coordinator to work with those assigned to the new churches

A. **What are the strategic initiatives?**
    The Field coordinator will serve as liaison between the Dept. of Missions and the newly assigned pastors.
    The Field Coordinator will ensure that the needs of the new churches are met in a timely manner.

B. **Accountability (who is responsible):**   The Director of Missions

C. **Milestones/Indicators:**
    Completion of 1st phase of School of Missions
    Church Planting Workshop to be held by 11/08
    New church(es) to be planted beginning 11/08

D. **Time frame:**
    Expectations and Job description for the position of Field Coordinator to be completed by 10/15/08.
    Appointment of Field Coordinator by 10/25/08

STRATEGIC PLANNING

Strategy # 2: Establish two new academy schools by 2010
We agreed to make assessment for two new schools.
Our aspiration is to start two new schools by 2010.
The goal:
To meet the strategic objective of providing sound education with a Biblical foundation
Actions required to meet strategic plan # 2
#1. Structural Identifications: We must identify the level at which the schools will be initially operated. We must also identify the infrastructural needs and the locations of the new schools.
What are the strategic initiatives?
A. For quality and excellence, and to meet governmental requirements as well as financial prudence, it would be best to initially operate the new schools at the elementary division.
B. Lease or erect a structure as new government regulations reject operating academy schools in church edifice.
C. Primarily focus on Rivercess and Margibi counties. If possibility does not exist focus on any of the churches within the vicinity of Monrovia.
Accountability (who is responsible):
The Local Pastors within the designated areas and the Director of Education with special assistant from the Administration of Kingdom Harvest Academy.
Milestones/Indicators:
A. Completion of assessment at the Tower Hills Fellowship in Lower Margibi and the two churches in River Cess County
B. Submission of recommendations to KHM Secretariat
C. Assessment and recommendations from other churches within the vicinity of Monrovia
Time frame:
Completion of all assessments by 12/08
Submission of all recommendations to the Secretariat by 03/09

Strategy # 2: Establish two new academy schools by 2010
We agreed to make assessment for two new schools.
Our aspiration is to start two new schools by 2010.
The goal:
To meet the strategic objective of providing sound education with a Biblical foundation
Actions required to meet strategic plan # 2
#2. Identification of Administrative staffs: The Secretariat in consultation with the Director of Education will hire the administrative staffs. The Administrator will directly hire all instructional and support staffs in collaboration with the local church leadership.
What are the strategic initiatives?
A. Primarily, the ideal candidates should come from within the KHM circle.
B. If no one from KHM is available, seek qualified administrators from the community in which the school is to be operated.
Accountability (who is responsible):
The Secretariat, Director of Education and the Local church Pastors of the community in which the school is to be operated.
Milestones/Indicators:
The Director of Education to set criteria for qualification.
The Secretariat to develop job descriptions for all administrative staffs.
The Secretariat to hire & assign administrators.
Time frame:
Criteria for qualification to be ready by 12/08.
Job descriptions to be ready by 03/09
Administrators to be hired and assigned one month before the start of school

Strategy # 3: Operate KHM under sound financial management
The present financial set-up calls for a direct deposit of all funds collected and that all spending be done through the invoice system.
The goal:
Ensuring that every fund collected is properly accounted for and spent for the intended purpose so as to meet our strategic goal of properties acquisition, investment in farming projects, and putting in place a better incentive package to attract and retain qualified staffs at all levels of the organization.
Actions required to meet strategic plan # 3
A. Every local church to make monthly financial reports to congregation & quarterly reports to KHM Secretariat. B. All KHM schools to make quarterly financial reports to local school board and semi-annual financial reports to the Secretariat.
What are the strategic initiatives?
The secretariat to audit each report to ensure proper accountability and determine proper (NOT EQUAL) distribution or allocation of resources.
Accountability (who is responsible):
The Director of Finance
Milestones/Indicators:
A. Each local church to hire a full time book keeper. B. Each new church to deposit funds with Mother church for 6 months, then open own account.
Time frame:
Every church that does not have a bank account to open one by 10/08. Anytime a new church is established

Strategy # 4: Ensure that each entity is autonomous, self-financing, and self-propagating.
Undertake business ventures for self-sustainability. Acquired and cultivated farm lands. Use local tools to cultivate the acquired farm lands. Create the avenue for entrepreneurship.
The goal:
Keep our focus on local fund raising initiatives other than tithes and offerings. To keep the ministry solvent so that we can truly be a church planting movement that can adequately provide spiritual, educational, and medical supports within Liberia.
Actions required to meet strategic plan # 4
#1. Operate internet café and after school computer classes for the general public
What are the strategic initiatives?
A. Operate the café with a computer school after the normal academic session week days and 6am-9pm Saturdays. B. Keep equipments updated, & ensure proper maintenance. C. Strategize expansion of the café and school
Accountability (who is responsible):
The Administration of Kingdom Harvest Academy
Milestones/Indicators:
A. Shop around with internet service providers for best options & services. B. Set up café when container arrives from USA C. Hire caretakers and teachers D. Expand café and invest into another business
Time frame:
A. Deadline for window shopping and recommendations for ISP is August 25, 2008. B. Start the operation of the café one week after all equipments are set up and tested. C. Within one year of operation, percentage of proceed should be invested into another business.

STRATEGIC PLANNING

Strategy # 4: Ensure that each entity is autonomous, self-financing, and self-propagating.
Undertake business ventures for self-sustainability. Acquired and cultivated farm lands. Use local tools to cultivate the acquired farm lands. Create the avenue for entrepreneurship.
The goal:
Keep our focus on local fund raising initiatives other than tithes and offerings. To keep the ministry solvent so that we can truly be a church planting movement that can adequately provide spiritual, educational, and medical supports within Liberia.
Actions required to meet strategic plan # 4
#2. Operate rental car service and do regular maintenance every three months and specific maintenance as needed on the cars
What are the strategic initiatives?
A. The Secretariat to rent one of the three donated vehicles weekly B. Praise & DuPort Rd to rent their assigned vehicles at least twice a week C. Each entity to ensure proper maintenance of vehicles
Accountability (who is responsible):
The Secretariat The deacons and Elders at Praise & DuPort Rd
Milestones/Indicators:
A. Shipment received from USA and cleared from Port of Monrovia B. Set up guidelines for rental service C. Hire drivers D. Within one year of operation, percentage of proceed should be invested into another business.
Time frame:
A. If all goes well, shipment should be received and cleared anytime before 12/31/08 B. Guidelines for rental service by all entity concerned should be ready by 10/31/08 C. Drivers should be hired when vehicles are ready D. Percentage of proceed should be invested into another business by 12/31/09
Strategy # 4: Ensure that each entity is autonomous, self-financing, and self-Propagating.
Undertake business ventures for self-sustainability. Acquired and cultivated farm lands. Use local tools to cultivate the acquired farm lands. Create the avenue for entrepreneurship.
The goal:
Keep our focus on local fund raising initiatives other than tithes and offerings. To keep the ministry solvent so that we can truly be a church planting movement that can adequately provide spiritual, educational, and medical supports within Liberia.
Actions required to meet strategic plan # 4
#3. Every local church should identify and operate either a farm or another project as an additional source of income.
What are the strategic initiatives?
A. Each local church to raise the money, (if farming) acquire and cultivate the land.

B. Identify, plant and harvest the crop; develop marketing strategy and sell produce.
C. 40% of proceed to be given to the Secretariat for church planting purposes and 60% to be used by the local church as desired.
Accountability (who is responsible):   The Senior Pastors and leadership team of each local church.
Milestones/Indicators:
A. Each local church to identify project and submit proposal to the Secretariat
B. For farming projects, each church to acquire land before the farming season
C. Each local church to submit proposal of how funding for the project will be raised to the Secretariat
D. Fund raising programs to be held by each church solely for the identified project.
E. Land to be cultivated and crop planted during the specific crop farming season
F. Develop marketing strategy and initiatives before harvesting & selling the produce
Time frame:
A. Projects proposals to be submitted to Secretariat by 10/31/08
B. Farm lands to be either identified and/or acquired by 11/30/08
C. Fund raising proposals to be submitted to Secretariat by 08/30/08
D. Fund raisers to be held between 09/01/08 to 11/30/08
E. Land to be cultivated and crop planted during the specific crop farming season in 2009.
F. Marketing initiatives and strategy to be developed by 02/15/09.

BIBLIOGRAPHY

Addleson, M. "Resolving the Spirit and Substance of Organizational Learning." *Journal of Organizational Change Management* 9, no. 1 (1996): 32. Retrieved November 18, 2006 from the University of Phoenix ERR page.

Allison, M. "Into the Fire: Boards and Executive Transitions." *Nonprofit Management & Leadership* 12, no. 4 (2002).

Back, K. M. "Project Performance: Implications of Personality Preferences and Double Loop Learning." *Journal of American Academy of Business*, 4, no. 1 (2004): 292, 6p.

Banerji, P. and V. Krishnan. *Leadership and Organization Development Journal* 21, no. 8 (2000): 405.

Bass, B. M. *Leadership and Performance Beyond Expectations*. New York, NY: Free Press, 1985.

Bass, B. M. *Bass & Stogdill's Handbook of Leadership*. 3rd ed. New York: Free Press, 1990.

Barclay, W. "A Comparison of Paul's Missionary Preaching and Preaching to the Church." In *Apostolic History and the Gospel. biblical and Historical Essays Presented to F. F. Bruce.* Exeter: The Paternoster Press, 1970.

Becerra-Fernandez, I., A. Gonzalez, and R. Sabherwal. *Knowledge Management: Challenges, Solutions and Technologies.* Upper Saddle River, NJ: Pearson Education, Inc., 2004.

Block, P. *Flawless Consulting.* 2nd ed. John Wiley & Sons Inc., 2002.

Burke, R. "Culture's Consequences: Organizational Values, Satisfaction and Performance. *Empowerment in Organizations*, 3(2) (1995): 19–24. Retrieved November 18, 2006 from EBSCOhost database.

Burns, M. K. "Using Curriculum-Based Assessment in Consultation: A Review of Three Levels of Research." *Journal of Educational & Psychological Consultation* 15 no.1 (2004): p63, 16p.

Conger, J. "Charismatic and Transformational Leadership in Organizations: An Insider's Perspective on These Developing Streams of Research." *Leadership Quarterly* 10, no. 2 (1999): 145.

Dalton, A. "Human Capital." ***p.m.Network*** 20(8) (2006): 70–75. Retrieved November 18, 2006 from EBSCOhost database.

Davis, M. et al. "Reflecting on the experience of inter-viewing online: perspectives from the Internet and HIV study in London." *AIDS Care* 16, no. 8 (2004): p944, 9p.

Drucker, P. F. "What Makes an Effective Executive?" *Harvard Business Review* 82, no. 6 (2004).

Ekman, B. and E. Giangregorio. "Establishing Truly Peak Performing Teams-Beyond Metaphoric Challenges. *Human Resource Management International Digest*, 11 (3), 3 (2003).

Fernandez, I., A. Gonzalez, and R. Sabherwal. **Knowledge** *Management: Challenges, Solutions, and Technologies*. Upper Saddle River, NJ: Prentice-Hall, 2004.

Gautschi, T. F. "How to Work with a Micro-Manager." **Design News** 49(9), 156 (1993). Retrieved November 18, 2006 from EBSCOhost database.

Gecker, R. "You Better Recognize." *Business Source Premier* 36, no. 9 (2003).

Goldman, A. I. *Knowledge in a Social World*. Oxford: Oxford University Press, 1999.

Gray. *Project Management: The Managerial Process*. 2nd edition. New York: McGraw Hill 2002.

Greco, M. et al. "Evaluation of a Clinical Governance Training Programme for Non-Executive Directors of NHS Organisations." *Quality in Primary Care Radcliffe Medical Press* 12, no. 2 (2004): 119, 9p.

Happ, M. B. et al. "Event Analysis Techniques." *Advances in Nursing Science* 27, no. 3 (2004): 239, 10p;

Harrison, B. "The Nature of Leadership: Historical Perspectives & the Future. *Journal of California Law Enforcement* 33(1) (1999): 24–30.

Kanter, R. M. "The Middle Manager as Innovator." *Harvard Business Review* 82, no. 7 (2004).

King, C. R. "Cautionary Notes on Whiteness and Sport Studies." *Sociology of Sport Journal* 22, no. 3 (2005): 397, 12p. AN 18184098. Retrieved July 23, 2006 from EBSCOhost database.

Kirby, G. R. and J. R. Goodpaster. *Thinking*. 3rd ed. Upper Saddle River, NJ: Prentice Hall, 2002.

Kopeikina, L. "Lead with Clarity: How to Make Effective Decisions." *Cost Engineering* 48, no. 2 (2006): 7–8, 2p.

Kosmin, B. A. and A. Keysar. *American Religious Identification Survey*. 2009.

Kreman, L. J. *Employee Empowerment Journal of Property Management* 68, no. 3 (2003).

Lawlor, A. "Week Three Lecture." LDR/711. Course-Materials Newsgroup. 2006. Retrieved April 26, 2006 from the UOP Doctoral site.

Lawlor, A. "Week Four Lecture." LDR/711. Course-Materials Newsgroup. 2006. Retrieved May 3, 2006 from the UOP Doctoral site.

McKernon, S. "The PoMo in You." *NZ Marketing Magazine* 21(1) (2002): 10.

Mika, V. S. et al. "The ABCs of Health Literacy." 28, no. 4 (2005): 351–357. Retrieved November 2, 2006 from ProQuest database.

McGill, Tanya. "The Effect of End User Development on End User Success." *Journal Of Organizational And End User Computing* 16(1) (2004): 41–58. Retrieved December 14, 2004 from ABI/INFORM Global database. Document ID: 533172481.

Moser, P. K. and A. Vander Nat, eds. *Human Knowledge: Classical and Contemporary Approaches*. 3rd ed. New York: Oxford University Press, 2002.

Olson, D. T. *The American Church in Crisis: Groundbreaking Research on a National Database of Over 200,000 Churches*. Zondervan. 2008.

Organization and Management Theory Conference Paper Abstracts. *Academy of Management Proceedings* (2003): p1, 77p.

Parks, B. "The World of Business in 2020." *Business 2.0* 5(3) (2004): 119–124.

Pauleem, D. "Leadership in a Global Virtual Team: An Action Learning Approach." *Leadership & Organization Development Journal* 24, no. 3 (2003): 153.

Phillips, J. "Paradigms of reading: Relevance Theory and Deconstruction/Close Reading: The Reader (Book). "*European Journal of English Studies* 8, no. 1 (2004): 138–144, 7p. AN 14734340. Retrieved July 24, 2006 from EBSCOhost database.

Power, M. "Anti-Racism, Deconstruction and Overdevelopment." *Progress in Development Studies* 6, no. 1 (2006): p24–39, 16p. Retrieved July 23, 2006 from EBSCOhost database.

Ray, T. "Cultural Sensitivity a Must in Global World." *Montgomery Advertiser.* (2004). Retrieved November 14, 2006 from www.montgomeryad-vertiser.com.

Rezak, C. J. *Playing for Keeps* 58, no. 10 (2004): p93–94, 2p.

Ruggiero, V. R. *Beyond Feelings: A Guide to critical thinking.* 7th ed. Boston: McGraw Hill, 2004.

Sarup, M. **An Introductory Guide to Post-Structuralism and Postmodernism**. Athens, GA: University Georgia Press, 1993.

Schaeffer, L. D. "The Leadership Journey." *Harvard Business Review* 80, no.10 (2002).

Schwarze, S. and H. Lape. *Thinking Socratically: Critical Thinking About Everyday Issues.* Upper Saddle River, NJ: Prentice Hall, 2001.

Scott, W. R. and G. F. Davis. *Organizations and Organizing: Rational, Natural, and Open Systems Perspectives.* Prentice Hall. Pearson Education, Inc., 2007.

Stetzer, E. "Finding New Life for Struggling Churches." *Journal of the Southern Baptist Convention* February/ March Issue (2010).

Summers, D. J. et al. "Deconstructing the Organizational Behavior Text." *Journal of Management Education* 21(3) (1997): 343–360.

Tichy, N. M. and E. Cohen. *Why Are Leaders Important in Business Leadership: A Jossey-Bass Reader.* San Francisco: Jossey-Bass, 2003.

Weiskittel, P. "The Concept of Leadership." *ANNA Journal*, 26(5) (1999): 467.

Whalen, T. and S. Samaddar. "Post-Modern Management Science: A Likely Convergence of Soft Computing and Knowledge Management Methods. *Human Systems Management,* 20(4) (2001): 291.

Wren, D. A. *The Evolution of Management Thought.*5th ed. New York: John Wiley & Sons, 2004.

Wycoff, J. *The Big Ten Innovation Killers and How to Keep Your Innovation System Alive and Well.* 2004. Retrieved May 25, 2008 from http://www. thinksmart.com.

www.ingramcontent.com/pod-product-compliance
Lightning Source LLC
LaVergne TN
LVHW091530070526
838199LV00001B/7